INTO YOUR HANDS

Andrew Clitherow is Director of Training for the Diocese of Blackburn and a Canon Residentiary of Blackburn Cathedral. At the time of writing this book, he was the vicar of a busy suburban parish in Lancaster where he worked with others to set up a Retreat and Renewal Centre for those living in Urban Priority Areas. In addition to parochial ministry, he has also worked in schools, having been at one time Chairman of the School Chaplains' Conference.

INTO YOUR HANDS

Prayer and the Call to Holiness
in Everyday Ministry and Life

––––––––––

Written for the parish priest and for
anyone in a position of spiritual leadership

Andrew Clitherow

Published in Great Britain in 2001 by
Society for Promoting Christian Knowledge
Holy Trinity Church
Marylebone Road
London NW1 4DU

British Library Cataloguing-in-Publication Data

A catalogue record for this book is available
from the British Library

ISBN 0–281–05353–7

Typeset by Wilmaset Ltd, Wirral, Merseyside
Printed in Great Britain by
Antony Rowe Ltd, Chippenham, Wiltshire

CONTENTS

In gratitude to my guardian angel
and to all those with whom it has been
a privilege to share the journey thus far.

FOREWORD

The compilers of a recent survey concluded that clergy are at the very top of the 'job satisfaction' list in Britain. This does not surprise me. The privileges of ordained ministry, whether working in a parish or community setting, are many and varied. The responsibility of contributing to the life and welfare of a locality, in the name of Jesus Christ, is at the very heart of the ordained person's response to God.

Other surveys in the last couple of years, however, have also revealed the stress and tensions within many clerical lives and those who share their homes. Hierarchs have tried to ease life by shaping various ministry development reviews and support systems, but much of day-to-day diaconal or priestly life demands determined perseverance and the consolations of prayer.

Andrew Clitherow's modesty in trying to set out the primary calling of the ordained minister today is encouraging, approaching the subject, he says, not as one who gets things right but who knows what it is like to get things wrong. He is conscious of the creative role of the pastor and of the shadows that often surround this creativity. I commend his work to you, not least his emphasis on prayer and meditation. He is perceptive, knowing both challenge and danger, and writes with the wisdom of Abba Macarius who reminds us not to lose ourselves in words but to 'spread out our hands and pray Lord, as thou wilt and as thou knowest best, have mercy'.

The Rt Revd and Rt Hon Richard Chartres, Bishop of London

INTRODUCTION

Stress in Christian ministry often arises out of the false assumption that we can preserve our lives when in fact we cannot. Vision is something we discover when we cease to concentrate on self-preservation and begin to comprehend the way God sees us and our destiny. Holiness then comes as an unexpected gift when we understand that the harmony of our life's symphony is to be found in the discord as much as anywhere, as the Spirit of God seeks to pursue the purposes of his love in us.

The calling of a parish priest is unique. While it shares undoubted areas of overlap with other forms of spiritual leadership and similarities with other vocations, there is little that comes close.

Within this experience there are times of great personal joy, celebration and spiritual fullness that can be had nowhere else. To exercise the role of a priest in any given situation is always an immense privilege. This is particularly the case when we realize that we have helped others to find, develop or express their spirituality.

Not long ago a group of six Canadians visited our church. They came without warning. Six remaining children of nine. They had been to France to see the recently discovered grave of a brother whose plane had been shot down in the Second World War. They were now on their way home but had made time to see the place where their parents had been married prior to emigrating. We stood together at the chancel step and remembered absent parents and loved ones while giving thanks for the eternal nature of love. While I had not met them previously – and am unlikely ever to see them again – for a moment I was allowed direct access into their lives at a very deep level. They accepted my vocation and so allowed me to share in some of their innermost thoughts at a time when they stood on that very thin line which separates earth from heaven.

Parish priests are also very familiar with times of pain, confusion, loneliness and great stress when a feeling of loss of control spreads from the lives of others to ourselves. We struggle to avoid the hoops through which others expect us to jump. Concentrating all our energies on spiritual, pastoral and managerial acrobatics, the danger is that we cease to live in harmony with our surroundings and with God. Home life, the quest for holiness and working for the wholeness of others become compartmentalized and the various needs compete against each other in unnecessary confrontation.

With this fragmentation – together with the pressures of social conformity, the perceptions of others and the need to be a focus of spirituality within a community – can come a sense of isolation. Yet when seeking help at such times we can discover that the very act of trying to explain our particular situation is fraught with difficulties. For only those with special insight into the life of the priest can offer any realistically constructive empathy.

The Church at national and local levels has become much more aware in recent years of the need to provide professional support for those in parochial ministry. There are systems in place which can provide the environment and expertise required when from time to time matters run away with us, and in some way or other we lose the control we need to remain balanced in our outlook, work and lifestyle. Help can be provided by friends, parishioners and colleagues, lay or ordained, often through collaborative ministry and ministry teams. It is not my intention, however, to look at how these structures can make support available, but rather to concentrate on those areas of life which the individual is called to manage mostly on his or her own. The parish priest – whether in group, team, cluster or traditional deanery organization – has prime responsibility for maintaining his or her own spiritual and emotional equilibrium, and this responsibility is heavy to bear.

At the heart of our ministry, however, lies the primary and often neglected call to holiness that others might see the face of Christ in and through us.

The degree of holiness expected of the spiritual leaders in other religions often stands in stark contrast to the expectations of those who lead at local level in the Church. An emphasis on activism, results and success can produce a form of discipleship that does not trespass too much on the demands and delights of the call to be holy. Moreover, when the spiritual caste of a religion loses sight of its calling, there is a real danger that the faith of the family of believers becomes diluted, unattractive, undemanding and good only for the short term and superficial.

Given the way the work of the parish priest has developed over recent years, there is perhaps a need today for a redefinition of his or her role. In the current market place of belief systems, the pre-eminence once given to the tradition and inherited tenets of the Christian faith has gone. In reaction to this the Church has felt the need to adopt effective marketing and management techniques, although the implementation of these should not divert its spiritual leaders from their vocation to be people of prayer and spiritual depth.

I hesitate to write about such things myself, being only too aware of the inadequacies of my own spiritual life and ministry. I approach this subject therefore not as one who gets things right but as one who knows what it is like to get things wrong. As one who simply wishes to share some insights that may bring comfort to others who are facing similar challenges.

It is my hope, therefore, that this short book will be a companion to the parish priest and to others in positions of spiritual leadership both in the affirmation of existing ministries and also in the reassessment of priorities where this may be desired. I hope, also, that where appropriate it will challenge the reader to rediscover – probably for the most part through redefinition – the call to holy living that God gives to all Christians and in particular to those entrusted with positions of spiritual authority.

This is not an attempt to turn back the clock, encourage the wearing of monastic robes and refute the materialistic excesses of the modern world! It is, rather, a recollection that invariably God is more active in and through us than we realize, as our lives themselves become prayers. Holiness in everyday life, therefore, is not perhaps as elusive as we might sometimes suppose.

In our darkest times – which are frequently our most lucid – we may feel that we have ceased to have a prayerful ministry either because we do not any longer make real prayer a priority or, and this is far more likely, because we have forgotten the mechanics and processes of prayer.

In the face of such self-criticism it is worth remembering that authentic prayer is defined and governed by the processes of covenant love. This love is based upon a binding commitment between God and humanity which exists beyond both what the mind can tell and the heart can feel. When two people first fall in love with each other, there seems to be so much that needs to be said and in as many ways as possible. Given time and attention that love becomes so strong and deep that words become almost unnecessary. Eventually, it is in silence rather than speech that the two lovers are most intimate. Similarly, in covenant love this commitment begins first in the mind as a decision to follow God and later descends through the heart to the spirit where the believer is caught up – often unwittingly – in the love and life of God.

Sometimes we might think that our prayers have just become paralysed by the burdens of daily living. However, just as the current of love between two people continues to operate when their attention and energies are not directed specifically towards each other, so the covenant is sustained by the Spirit of God when we sometimes look the other way. Whereas infatuation produces feelings of guilt when thoughts are elsewhere, we know that the strength of covenant love is more than sufficient to cope with fecklessness and infidelity.

Covenant love between God and humanity does not depend upon external actions but internal disposition. The flood of words at conversion leads ultimately to a contemplative silence deep within the spirit where God is perceived to be in and through all things. Then to look beneath the surface of reality or beyond the horizon of human endeavour is to perceive the power and presence of God. If we remain true to our covenant relationship with God – regardless of whether we judge ourselves to be any good at living the Christian life or not – then the life of God and our lives are drawn inexorably together towards a point of final union.

At ordination a new relationship is formed within this covenant. In the early years there can be a laudable desire to expend most of one's energies on the marketing of both the benefits of share-holding and the possibility of long-term dividends for those who are prepared to buy in to the company of the kingdom of God! Later on this outlook may give way to a quiet acceptance of the need to concentrate more on being than doing, if we are to conform to the purposes of the love of God. Calling the world to join the church gives way to an understanding that it is in the world that the church is to be found – where God has been ceaselessly and tirelessly active long before we were born.

In between the former and latter forms of spiritual leadership lies much soul-searching when we can demand more of ourselves than does God. Here we have to learn to accept ourselves and our own shortcomings before we can accept the will of God. We do well to remember that as long as we continue to persevere with our calling, there is nowhere we can place ourselves which is either closer or further away from God. We make a mistake when by our own standards we describe ourselves as having 'drifted away' from God as if there is anywhere where we might be able to hide from him. What we often mean instead is that we have ceased to remember that he is with us.

This is not the same as the experience of the spiritual desert in which there is a particular absence of God for one of a number of reasons. It has more to do with a lack of perception of the continuous presence of Divine Love in all reality. In our preoccupation with many false dualisms which often separate the Christian faith from the world – seen, for example, in the way we sometimes fraudulently differentiate between the sacred and the secular – we lose sight of the Love that is always within and which constantly beckons from beyond.

Therefore, we need to beware of the misguided emphasis on 'being in love' – or 'making love' – in a society that concentrates to an unhealthy degree on the empirical and experiential. The whole of a person's life and ministry can be centred on the need to achieve certain goals which he or she believes will produce happiness and a purpose to justify his or her vocation. Yet in both the achievement of such a goal or in the frustration of having fallen short of it, there can remain a distinct absence of peace of mind and spirit. For covenant love is not concerned with an overriding quest for self-fulfilment by justification through good works. Instead, being sacramental by nature it reverses our understanding so that personal achievements – if we must describe them as such – come only as the fruit of a life whose primary aim is an unswerving commitment to see God in oneself and one's neighbour.

It is my hope, therefore, that through the pages that follow, the reader will be taken on a journey of prayer. Not a walk *to* love but *with* love. As a basis for this we will use the conversation as recorded by Mark that the brothers James and John had with Jesus on their last journey together on the road to Jerusalem. This passage is of particular significance as it contains a discussion that reveals the difference between the brothers' understanding of discipleship and that of Jesus. Here the quest for worldly power is challenged by the call to servanthood and self-sacrifice. Each chapter will reflect a different aspect of prayer arising out of this dialogue in an attempt to discern those constants in covenant love which are of particular importance for the Christian minister today. This is not to try and read the gospel as if it were written as some kind of textbook of models of discipleship and Christian ministry. Rather, it is an attempt to look behind the words of the written text to what we might discern as covenant love at work.

This road on which we will travel is well worn by previous generations of pilgrims. No doubt we have been this Way before. Yet familiar paths can hold unexpected surprises – even for the very experienced – when prayer and love combine to lead us to forgotten or as yet unappreciated truths. Such revelations as we might come across will not only encourage and delight but also demand something more of the depths of covenant love to which we have yet to surrender ourselves. For while we feel the security of the path beneath our feet, we are at the same time invited to discover that sense of eternity that comes when we let go completely in the self-offering of prayer and love. To tread this path is a risky business, but if we are not prepared to chance such naked vulnerability then a society that yearns to make sense of God – where pilgrimages are taken not only on foot but in cars, trains and aeroplanes – is likely to be deprived of something of the opportunity to share in the ecstasy of incarnate love.

James and John, the sons of Zebedee, came forward to him and said to him, 'Teacher, we want you to do for us whatever we ask of you.' And he said to them, 'What is it you want me to do for you?' And they said to him, 'Grant us to sit, one at your right hand and one at your left, in your glory.' But Jesus said to them, 'You do not know what you are asking. Are you able to drink the cup that I drink, or be baptised with the baptism that I am baptised with?' They replied, 'We are able.' Then Jesus said to them, 'The cup that I drink you will drink; and the baptism with which I am baptised, you will be baptised; but to sit at my right hand or at my left is not mine to grant, but it is for those for whom it has been prepared.'

(Mark 10.35–40)

Andrew Clitherow, priest and sinner

1

The Prayer of the Beating Heart

'Teacher, we want you to do for us whatever we ask of you.'

(Mark 10.35b)

The story is reaching its climax as the disciples talk with Jesus. The right time – the *kairos* – had come. Jesus was soon to confront the religious institution and political establishment in Jerusalem. What was about to happen was to be 'crucial' (that is, centred on the cross) to the establishment of the kingdom through the redemptive suffering of the One who came to be called the Son of God.

By this time, the disciples had been with Jesus for approximately three years. There would have been times of exhilaration as they saw the purposes of God unfold. On other occasions, in the face of fierce opposition, they must have wondered whether they had made a dreadful mistake. At such times, the fishing boats of the Sea of Galilee and a settled life with family and friends must have offered a more attractive lifestyle compared with a nomadic existence and a leader whose claims were so outlandish they were Christ-like. That is, they can only have been made by the Anointed One of God who was expected to restore the rule of God and the fortunes of the Jewish people.

From the text of Mark, the disciples – often portrayed as being slow to comprehend the message of Jesus – were unaware at this stage of the exact nature of the events about to take place. It is more than likely, however, that they sensed the

1

danger that the teaching of Jesus would bring once they had entered Jerusalem. They would have known that his claims – made in the religious and political heart of the nation at a time when it was packed for the Passover – might mean that he would be taken from them for ever. Hence the request.

This question, though, was different from others that had been asked earlier. It displays among other things great courage, commitment and determination. James and John were not asking to know the meaning of a particular parable (Mark 4.10ff) nor were they confused by the way the teaching of Jesus seemed to overturn their traditional and accepted values (Mark 10.26). Coming as it does after the third time Jesus had warned the disciples of his impending death, this request arises from a plan devised by the two to take over leadership of the group following their Master's death. Yet it would appear that the nerve of the brothers was not balanced by an equal amount of integrity. There was a certain dishonesty about their request. For James and John were asking for power. They wanted to have control over others and ultimately over God. Here, surfacing among the most trusted followers of Jesus, was the sin of pride which subsequently was to become a great stumbling block for the Church.

Such rebellious feelings, though, will not be unfamiliar today to those whom God has called into his service. The place where we make our demands for power is also frequently at the point of access, namely in prayer. Sometimes we can see the cross that lies ahead for us and we feel the need to take control. To force our own agenda. To have our own way. How swift and adept we are to read into our prayers the justification for the answers we wish to receive. We claim the authority of God for our own ends, preferring to become deaf to the Word rather than hear the unpalatable response that will thwart our dreams for power and success. While we think we are serving Christ, we pull at the strings of a puppet god of our own invention, jerking in favour to the pull of our ambition.

Our experience is that prayer is often very hard work! It does not always come easily. After a period of struggle we can wonder why we cannot have instant access and communication. We ignore the fact that despite the seemingly unlimited access to God that Christ gives to the believer today, the prayer of covenant love has to be founded on respect by both parties for each other. A lack of respect in prayer indicates that we have broken the covenant. At this point we may be sure that we are pursuing our own agreement, not with God but with ourselves.

Prayer and the problem of communication

Those who have made major lifestyle changes in response to a vocation to the ordained ministry, and are constantly assessing and reassessing their commitment to live out the gospel, may well in this instance envy James and John their direct access to Jesus. If only his disciples today who have also embarked on a journey – both spiritual and physical – which has isolated them from a more straightforward and comfortable existence, could simply sidle up to Jesus and ask for more power, greater wisdom, increased understanding, more faith, and at least some patience! There are few who would not gladly risk his wrath and rebuke if they, too, could also present their requests in such a direct manner.

Sadly, communication with him is not as direct as it is with those with whom our mortal coils share physical space and the temporal sphere. Hence the need to pray and to work at praying. And the function of this prayer is not merely to express our frustration and make unreasonable demands but also, and more importantly, to concentrate on being with Christ – to share his company – along the way. Anyone who has tried it soon becomes aware that the path of prayer is neither direct nor simple and is frequently fraught with difficulty. While prayer can involve feelings of spiritual fullness and the sense of being loved forever, it can also bring experiences of loneliness and confusion. Moreover, it is not unusual to discover the difficult outnumbering the good times! Yet prayer remains the principal medium by which we converse with the Risen Christ. And speak with Christ we must if our spirits are to live, our faith grow and we are to work as and where he wills. Inevitably, therefore, as we are impelled to keep in constant touch with the One who is the source of all authentic love, we are driven to our knees. Then we regularly have confirmed for us the truth that if direct speech is an inexact science, effective prayer can be even more elusive.

Comfort comes from the knowledge that there are very few Christians and certainly no saints in the history of the Church who have not struggled with prayer. As we read about their lives we can see that they, too, experienced occasions of great spiritual enlightenment – of peace and a sense of the Divine presence – which seem to come as a gift from Lover to beloved. They also experienced arid spiritual deserts which had to be crossed. Anyone who has crossed the desert knows from experience that it is during such times that the most important lessons are often learned about the nature of God, humanity and our service of Christ. Furthermore, whether our personal spirituality lives or dies depends largely upon our reaction to the realization from time to time that the streams of living water that regularly gush life into our spirits, and through us to others, have all but dried up.

The desert produces one of the most demanding situations that the spiritual leader has to face, for the life of a priest is usually understood to be public property and he or she rarely travels without the company of others. His or her life and faith are there for all to see, discuss and dissect. Moreover, it is not difficult for others to take the temperature of the spiritual life of a priest. Preaching always seems less stressful and more effective when the spiritual life is going well. When it is not, there is a frightening feeling of nakedness when the taste of sand is discovered in the mouth and it is both too hot in the day and too cold at night. At times like this, honesty can be elusive. While we might be prepared to admit to ourselves that we have stumbled into a spiritual desert, there are many reasons why we dare not admit this publicly. Instead, the leader pretends that everything is fine. But the pretence can become permanent if the cause of the problem is not addressed. Such pretence swiftly leads to spiritual dehydration and death.

This dryness of the spirit is vividly expressed by the psalmist:

I am poured out like water,
    and all my bones are out of joint;
my heart is like wax;
    it is melted to my breast;
my mouth is dried up like a potsherd,
    and my tongue sticks to my jaws;
you lay me in the dust of death.
                    (Psalm 22.14–15)

Yet, if we persevere, the experience of spiritual exhaustion leads unexpectedly to renewed strength. The psalm ends on a note of faith and hope. So – against the pre-Pentecost odds – did the lives of James and John. Not long after they made their famous request they had no choice but to discover how to maintain their faith when it seemed that the reason for it had gone. The brothers, in common with every generation of those who would seek after God, were forced to face the great paradox of the life of prayer as they faced the absence of Jesus in apparent defeat. Namely, that in times of faithlessness one must have faith in order to have hope.

Both in the heat and the cold we are bidden to return to God. If prayer is simply regarded as something to be used only when a favour or a solution to a problem is required – whether this is to do with funding for the church roof or a particularly demanding parishioner – this is clearly an abuse of the relationship we have been called to enjoy with God through Christ. Sadly, in a busy life where increasing emphasis is placed upon reports, results and the need for a successful religion, it is not uncommon for daily prayer to be regarded as a sacred yet largely irrelevant ritual.

Generally speaking, priests are the only people in a parish who are paid to pray. But the demands of the work, the false expectations of others and the fallibility of the individual often mean that the priest can end up paying more attention to peripheral matters than to his or her prayers. The result is that our prayer begins and ends with ourselves rather than with God. We ask that God will change externals while forgetting that the Christian path of prayer has always begun with a journey of inner transformation and empowerment. Walter Hilton (Park, 1998) tells us: 'Don't think that God is just somewhere "out there", God is as close as your own soul, seek God within yourself. If you wish to know God, know yourself.' In that it is only in finding God that we discover our true selves, we – priests in particular – have to come to terms with the often shallow people we have become. As the immanent God takes us to new depths of self-understanding and acceptance, it is from here that the Spirit gives us the strength and vision to journey outwards in relation to others and to the One who is beyond. This is not to deny a person his or her personal history of how they have become who they are. Rather, it is to understand humanity's potential anew with the clarity of objectivity that comes from the knowledge that everyone has been created and called to be 'in relationship' with the Creator.

The observation of St Augustine that our hearts are restless until they find their rest in God is pertinent for any generation which lays claim to spiritual maturity while remaining ill at ease with itself. We are very aware that so much of our understanding of ourselves in relation to our environment – and the peace of prayer is only found when harmony is achieved between these two – depends upon our meeting the ground of ourselves, the basis of our life. Prayer for power over others is based on the misunderstanding that change comes primarily from the alteration of externals. Instead, real power for life is to be found in the inner spiritual reorientation that prayer provides. Experiencing the peace this produces, we then cease to be at odds with those who are around us and – as the Spirit of unconditional love is released from within – are set free to serve them.

The prayers of the priest therefore provide not 'peace from' (escapism) but 'peace among' (living and witnessing amidst) the rigours of work in an urban priority area, the pressures of a city-centre ministry, the demands of rural parishes or the false respectability of suburbia, and so on. If we are reluctant to dig this deep in prayer, the Way that Jesus offers is rapidly reduced to a religion of the mind that fails to reach the heart. This, in turn, can lead us to see Christian leadership in terms of being respectable, ordained business people rather than those who are driven by the often untidy demands of radical love.

So it is our business, daily, to return to talk with Christ along the way.

The importance of returning to Christ in prayer

The following words of Thomas à Kempis encourage us to face in the right direction: 'Blessed be Thy Name, O Lord, forever (Psalm 113.2) who has willed that this temptation and tribulation should come upon me. I cannot escape it, but must needs flee to Thee, that Thou mayest help me, and turn it to my good.'

This is not to suggest that every problem is necessarily willed on us by God. However, when life is full of pain and makes little sense, the spiritual leader needs not only to cry out against feelings of God-forsakenness but also to force him- or herself into creative dialogue with the One who is the source of the call to service in the first place. When life becomes hard and suffering appears to be illogical the temptation is to give up on prayer. Spiritual engagement is substituted by cerebral exercises devoid of God which will never provide the 'answer' to our problems. At times such as these it is easy to become subservient to a fake spirituality of self-direction usually away from the source of discomfort and the healing love of God we were meant to share with those in pain. We do this instead of concentrating on the need to continue to pursue a life of self-giving love in which all things 'work together for good for those who love God, who are called according to his purpose' (Romans 8.28).

So, what form should this dialogue of prayer take? How do we call to God in faith for help with our faithlessness? If we look for God in the ground of our being, will we end up talking to ourselves, this being just another form of pride or false assent to the lust for power of the self?

One of the most common reasons why a person's prayer life dries up is because 'we have let ourselves slip into forgetting God even while we pray' (Temple, 1994). The way in which people often enter a church to pray is symptomatic in the West of a failure to understand the demands which are made by the God of love. There is often scant recognition of the Divine as warranting awe and wonder. Respect for the Creative Source of authentic love is often lost because of a self-consciousness that would rather regard liturgy as live entertainment. As Christians today search for ways to market the faith that are meaningful, the reductionist finds it difficult to cope with the irrationality of the love of God.

In the New Testament the most common word for worship is *proskuneo*, meaning literally 'to come forward to kiss'. Prayer – above all else – is concerned with finding a unity of being within a relationship that is based upon the love of the Creator for creation, of Father or Mother for son or daughter. The one who prays is far more likely to find an oasis in the spiritual desert if the laws of love rather than those of religion are applied. For love speaks of holding on unconditionally even to that which we do not understand and may not even like for a while, whereas religion so often finds a way to let go of that which is different

and threatening. Praying is like loving. From a true understanding and acceptance of the self comes the power to love
another. In true love there is no condemnation for simply being
oneself. No emotional cul-de-sac from which we cannot escape.
Every wrong turn becomes an opportunity to find the better
way. But the way of authentic love – where even unacceptable
feelings and actions once faced, shared and understood can be
incorporated into a stable and strong relationship – above all
depends upon and demands honesty on a daily basis from those
in a covenantal relationship. This is hard. It is much easier at
times to go and hide for fear of confrontation and rejection.
Hence the need for pretence which immediately introduces
artificiality into the relationship. Then suddenly infidelity –
previously regarded as unthinkable – becomes a present possibility if not an attractive alternative to facing up to the processes
of love.

Honesty in prayer is therefore of paramount importance. We
are not only to share our innermost secrets with God, but if we
are to remain on the journey with him, we have to be honest
with ourselves. Honesty asks us to admit that sometimes we feel
our faith has failed, and in creative dialogue to look at this and
move on to what will probably be a personal faith of greater
strength and realism. So when love is hot we return to celebrate
our union with God in prayer and when love grows cold we
return to the subject and object of our desires for warmth,
reassurance, meaning and strength. Perhaps, therefore, it is no
coincidence that in an age when the continuance of human
loving relationships in the West is under so much pressure –
where failure is often followed by fragmentation – the maintenance of constancy in prayer is so difficult.

During conversion – involving the beginning of a process by
which changes are made in the way a person thinks – the
disposition of the heart frequently takes precedence over that of
the mind. Conversion, in this sense, is like falling in love. There
is often a sudden passion for intimacy with God. To make love

with God. The convert can be almost consumed by an inward desire to pray as the Holy Spirit – thwarted in the depths of self-denial for so long – rushes to the surface. But when the headiness of emotions inevitably subsides he or she can easily be confused into thinking that God is moving away. The experiences that were the origins of joy cannot be conjured up again in quite the same way. At best this can leave the new believer feeling incomplete. At worst he or she might even begin to doubt their ability to love at all. Whereas communication was never a problem before, misunderstandings arise as more of the make-up of both partners – Divine and human – is revealed. This, however, is not a sign that love has become shallow but rather that it is becoming deeper.

At the beginning it is falsely assumed that prayer comes naturally. Later there comes a dawning understanding that prayer – like loving – is an art to be practised, functioning as it does at many different levels at any one time. The passion of the natural urges gives way to gentleness and sensitivity as the newly loved learns not to be threatened by what might erroneously be regarded as the disinterest of the Other. The physical side of love is but the expression of the much deeper – and more important – spiritual side. Love, then, is about loyalty, even – or especially – when we feel like being disloyal. It is at this point that emotional love has to function alongside rational commitment and fidelity. While not as attractive as the first flush of love, the daily round and common task of a relationship need not be devoid of an excitement and pleasure that is all-embracing.

The sculpture by Rodin entitled 'The Kiss' symbolizes the deepening of love once the heady days of early romance are past. The youthfulness of the figures is contrasted by a great maturity of loving. Knowledge of love is gained not so much by years of experience but by a willingness to be open and direct. The figures are strong and yet gentle; close and sensitive they communicate at a level beyond words. They enjoy a naked embrace, bodies bared of clothes, lives bared of pretence, spirits bared of evil. It is an embrace of limitless love and grace, beyond the space of limbs entwined and the time of quickened hearts. A love that ascends and descends into the very source of life which is God.

Mother Mary Clare of the Convent of the Incarnation, Oxford (1988) tells us that 'the simplicity of prayer is naked love'. It is this 'naked embrace' that needs to form the basis of our prayer life if on our journey in communion with Christ, we are to feel and enjoy his presence. When we make irrational requests or wish to put God at our disposal it is often because we have been ashamed to be naked in his presence. From time to time, our self-assertion can turn to an arrogant pride that threatens the integrity of our relationship with others and with God. To stand naked before God every day is to know his healing love for our pain and fear. It is not so much to make love as to commit ourselves to a life of unrestricted love. Such vulnerability rests not on long and complicated supplication or even intimacy of spirit but upon an openness of heart. This can be achieved by regular times of prayer through the day as a result of which God and believer share in each other's breath and life. As we thus make our requests and listen to the voice of God whispering in the quiet recesses of our hearts, we allow the life-giving properties of the Spirit to energize our lives and ministry.

Moreover, at the same time as creature and Creator learn to breathe in time together their hearts beat increasingly in time to a unity of being and purpose.

The labour of love in terms of the life of prayer can be seen therefore in what we might call 'heartbeat prayers'. While other forms of prayer reflect other aspects of love in relationship, these beat ceaselessly according to a regular rhythm, rendering a person sufficiently pure in spirit to see God and sufficiently filled with the Spirit to live in union with him and with his creation. Their particular characteristics are as follows.

11

- *They happen automatically.* We could never live if all the time we were concentrating on our hearts beating. We do not even have to be aware of them most of the time. They are for the most part the silent source of life, of cleansing and empowering. Their vital importance is not matched by our conscious expectations of them. As we go about our day-to-day business we assume that the heart will continue to beat. We have few expectations of it and usually take it for granted. Yet without it, we would cease to exist.

  While there are many different ways of praying, the heartbeat prayer is there all the time. Without it the spiritual life is prone to suffocation. While this type of prayer is a fundamental part of a believer's rule of life, little conscious attention is paid to it. In a busy life of parochial ministry, a priest gains great assurance from a regular rhythm beating behind everything that he or she is doing.

  These prayers are usually uttered more out of a sense of duty than from desire. 'Flirts', we are reminded, 'never get anywhere with God, turning to him only when they are in the mood for self-gratification' (Torkington, 1987). To confuse love with instant pleasure is to substitute freedom with slavery.

- *They usually occur without feeling.* The occasions when we are aware of our hearts beating usually occur either when we are neglecting them in some way or if we are taking time to exercise in order to keep the muscle strong and fit. At other times we have no direct experience of them and they have no direct bearing upon our emotional lives.

  Similarly, just as loving does not rely upon a constant emotional extravagance, neither does praying. When prayer becomes dependent upon how we feel – when we pray only when we want to and regard prayer as good only when we feel better afterwards – we have manipulated it to be a source of spiritual self-gratification to be switched on and off at will. It is possible to become almost self-congratulatory in the utterance of endless prayers, as the self is whipped into a state of emotional frenzy. Outwardly this prayer may well be about the needs of the world but inwardly it has become a form of spiritual self-abuse. The absence of an emotional 'high' does not indicate an absence of the Spirit of prayer.

While there are undoubtedly times when the Spirit can affect the emotions very powerfully, and while it is not in any way wrong to express our emotions when we pray, prayer consists primarily of a person – either individually or corporately – becoming one with God at a much deeper level. Prayer, then, is seated in the human spirit from which the emotions may or may not be affected. It does not depend upon our own efforts but on our willingness to be energized by the Holy Spirit who makes prayer possible in the first place and whose conjunction with the human spirit is the essence of this activity (cf. 1 Corinthians 2.10–12). Moreover, as this kind of prayer develops so the need to use words is diminished: 'It is for your own sake, not for God's, that you put your prayers into words' (Temple, 1994).

It is, therefore, nothing other than a threat to the life of the human spirit when people give up on heartbeat prayers, assuming they are irrelevant because they cannot feel them working.

- *They have a regular rhythm.* This may be different between individuals but whatever rhythm is right – even an irregular heartbeat – it is maintained at all times. At any time we can check our health by taking our pulse and measuring the number of beats per minute.

  If prayer is to keep us in touch with God then the need for immediacy – experienced or not – comes as a result of the regular rhythm being maintained. In fact, when this takes place we can quickly discover as we go about our business that spiritual life is indeed being pumped around our systems as levels of perception are heightened, the right words come more easily and we work with apparent effortlessness. In the Church of England this rhythm has traditionally been maintained by the saying of the daily office in Morning and Evening Prayer. The habit is caught often – though by no means exclusively – in residential training when ordinands pray regularly together. The practice is maintained during the first years of parochial ministry when again the offices are said in the company of a training parish priest. But during the sudden isolation of a first incumbency the daily office can take a terrible beating. Recited almost for the sake of mere repetition, abandoned for its perceived ineffectiveness, squeezed out by the almost impossible demands of the diary, it survives against the odds.

As a rhythm of love, however, and without unrealistic expectations of its purpose it can not only empower the minister but also enable him or her to reach out in healing love to others. While in public the priest is bound to use only those offices that are authorized, in private he or she may use various alternatives with good effect. So long as the heartbeat takes place, it does not have to be identical all year round. A certain amount of thoughtful use of alternatives can help considerably in alleviating that boredom that can come from overfamiliarity.

The daily office can be said anywhere: in the parish church, in the study, kitchen or attic, sitting outside or in the car. While place is important, it is of course by no means essential to say the office in one place every time. The important thing is that it is said. Although, given the intercessory side to the prayers, it makes sense to continue the tradition of saying the office as much as possible in the parish church where certainly on Sundays – if not during the week as well – services are held for the members of the community the priest seeks to serve.

- *They have a regular timing.* Our hearts have to beat within a certain number of times per minute. They do not work by storing up beats and releasing them all in one go! The beats have to be spaced out, according to a regular rhythm in time.

If we do not put set times aside to be with our loved ones then very quickly we find that we have not seen them for days and our lives are often the poorer. This state of affairs also indicates the priority we are giving to cherishing the love we have been given. While the heartbeat is unnoticeable, time with a loved one of many years may also pass without particular comment, but the time spent together will nevertheless have been deeply beneficial.

While a priest will spend time with God in other essential ways – such as Bible study and meditation – and in different and less formal forms of prayer, time set aside for the heart to beat makes sure that the 'cares of the world, and the lure of wealth and the desire for other things' (Mark 4.19) do not take away the life that God longs to give. When these times of prayer are forced into daily schedules, life is not only reorientated around God but also grounded in love. Concern over peripheral matters rapidly diminishes and decisions about matters of principal importance become more straightforward. A priest then begins to live in the world without conforming to that part of it which speaks in terms of getting rather than giving, doing rather than being. In being prevented from meeting the demands of those things which are by nature essentially transitory, the priest takes his or her bearings from that which is eternal. Here a proper understanding and use by us of *chronos* makes possible the provision by God of *kairos*, which will be discussed in greater detail later.

However many times it is decided the heart should beat in prayer each day – and the minimum should be the morning and evening offices or equivalent[1] – other commitments should not be allowed to get in the way. While, generally speaking, it is well-nigh impossible to maintain a prayer life without some disruption, the principal aim is that the times of heartbeat prayer should scythe through the diary and the day's commitments. Only emergencies and occasions of great need take precedence. And if it is not possible to pray at exact times then as near as we can get to them will suffice. Given what has been said above about our expectations of this form of prayer, and the fact that the services have been written for us already, this is not an impossible discipline to follow.

- *They help to make our love strong.* As we have noted already, the strength in any loving relationship and its ability to deal with difficulties is to be found in the way in which the lives of the partners become intertwined. The individuality of the two is not taken away but rather heightened in this vital process of growing together. If this does not take place they remain – to a large degree – separate. Independence needs to give way to interdependence and an awareness of the needs of the other. Moreover, an understanding has to be developed of how best to receive and respond to the love that provides self-worth and purpose.

God as the author of perfect love and as the perfect lover cannot therefore be a figure of overbearing authority. Nor can he be the one who effortlessly holds all the answers to what we may perceive as our feeble questioning. Instead, God makes himself vulnerable and open to the process that it will take for the believer to come to know and live with him. We journey with him as disciples and friends, in humility, obedience and with a sense of worship, not as those who for fear of rejection dare not approach. We travel as accepted loved ones, as sons and daughters, brothers and sisters whose company and love he so eagerly seeks. For the love of God cannot be complete without our love. So it is that we travel with him.

Consequently, as we are not only to be honest but also genuine in our relationship with God and in our understanding of love, it will not be long before we discover that such unfashionable concepts as discipline, obedience, loyalty and duty are fundamental to a healthy spiritual life. If the saints in times past had in common an experience of the difficulty of prayer, they also shared an understanding that love involves that kind of commitment which leads to loyalty of heart and mind and devotion of life.

Whatever else they got wrong, James and John are correct in thinking that they were soon to have to carry on where their Lord and Master had left off. Following them have come countless generations of spiritual leaders of the Church at local, national and international level who have also been called to serve others so that the work and witness of Christ should be continued. However, this calling can be very demanding, involving a high degree of commitment and dedication, and the cost can be great. As the years go by and idealism gives way to harsh reality, the parish priest might from time to time find more than a musical resonance in the words of *Jesus Christ Superstar*, 'Then I was inspired, now I'm sad and tired'![2] At times such as these it can pay dividends to revisit the many techniques available that can help prayer to be both fresh and vibrant. Moreover, if a healthy heartbeat is maintained, then instead of becoming impaired by growing cynicism, it is likely that our vision of the kingdom will be grounded in the life of God more than ever before.

NOTES

1 To morning and evening prayer can be added midday prayer and compline.
2 From the rock musical *Jesus Christ Superstar* by Andrew Lloyd Webber and Tim Rice.

REFERENCES

T. Park, *The English Mystics*, SPCK, London, 1998, p. 26.

Mother Mary Clare, *The Simplicity of Prayer*, SLG Press, Oxford, 1988.

W. Temple, *Christian Faith and Life*, Mowbray Moorhouse Publishing (text 1931), 1994, p. 109.

Thomas à Kempis, *The Imitation of Christ*, Penguin, London, 1983.

D. Torkington, *Peter Calvay – Prophet*, Spennithorne Publications, Liverpool, 1987.

2

THE PRAYER OF TRUST

*'Grant us to sit, one at your right hand and one at your
left, in your glory.'*

(Mark 10.37)

There can be little doubt that the lives of James and John were
revivified by their journey with Jesus through Galilee and the
regions thereabouts and finally to Jerusalem. This request
betrays, however, a misunderstanding of the way ahead.

They had reduced their relationship with God to the level of
the pragmatic and achievable in terms of the agenda of the
world. They had not yet understood that in pain and sacrifice lie
a perfect form of love and a knowledge of the Perfect Lover
which is not available along any other route. So they settled for
second best. They agreed to the great deception which pride and
fear bring to discipleship, namely that they were going to do
God's will their way.

For a number of reasons the parish priest can also in time
become so ground down by seemingly relentless pressure that
subservience to the will of God is supplanted by a natural desire
to salvage some quality of life for oneself and one's family. We
feel that there is only so much that we can take and, when
visible results are scarce, we can at least subconsciously make
the decision that as long as we keep the church ticking over, we
are fulfilling our calling.

So it is that vocation to the priesthood, so sincerely felt and
nurtured during training, can in a parish be translated into

'the job of running a church'. The change from one to the other comes as soon as we cease to trust God to provide for our needs or we decide that we want more than he is prepared to give.

At the outset, having a vocation to be a priest can feel like a direct call to wander over one's own equivalent of the Galilaean hills, preaching in terms of the Sermon on the Mount, followed by a journey to the inner city to take on the civic and religious authorities on behalf of the urban poor!

'Keep to the dream but temper the idealism with practicality'[1] is good advice on which to ponder when beginning to encounter the harsh realities of parish-based ministry. Nevertheless, the realization that much of a priest's work today bears little resemblance to that picture of a disciple's life that we tend to conjure up from the gospel accounts can lead rapidly to disillusionment, even for those with their eyes wide open.

From a superficial understanding of the gospel story, we can cling to an unrealistic image of discipleship. We use it as a measure by which to congratulate or condemn both ourselves and our church for either having produced a Christ-centred community, or not. It is an unfair method of criticism, however, for a study of the life of the early Church as recorded in the New Testament and the letters of the early Fathers reveals from the beginning a number of theological conflicts and power struggles that were part and parcel of the growing pains of the Body of Christ. Rather than using the Bible to beat ourselves up both spiritually and morally, we should instead take some comfort from the fact that, as a careful reading of the text reveals, apart from a few minutes following Pentecost there probably never has been a time when the Church has not to some degree or other distorted the truth. Therefore if the Church is to continue to follow the Spirit and be led ever deeper in its understanding of God, it is reasonable to expect that pains of growth and development will be integral to this process.

This is not, however, to condone any kind of complacency

when faith and conduct fall short of that life to which God has called us.

Neither Jesus nor his disciples were, of course, members of a church as we would understand this today. Nevertheless, from the time that Jesus called his closest followers to leave their homes and accompany him for three years along the way, they had to learn the meaning of Christian community. Then, as now, this community contained a patchwork of personalities all at various stages of growth in the Christian life.

Vocation under pressure

In common with the disciples, neither priests nor people today come to the Church in a state of perfection. Instead, they join as those who, having repented and been forgiven, have embarked on a lifelong commitment to grow in faith and love. If, though, we are to be committed to the sanctification of the Church in the present, there are errors common to every generation of Christians that need to be avoided. The diversity – on the road to Jerusalem with Jesus both then and now – that the Christian community can do without comes when priests and people decide to pursue their own agendas which are in clear conflict with the way of the cross.

Let me give two examples of how the exciting, innovative and unpredictable breath of the Spirit can be reduced to the gasp of the predictably mundane.

The first is that while to begin with there is an admission of a need for healing for the individual, the process by which this is pursued becomes forgotten as the busyness of being a church member takes over. Committees, good works and fundraising – while necessary and positive contributions in themselves – can become the *raison d'être* of religion. The need of the institution to survive becomes the all-embracing concern. Spiritual growth is measured by Sunday attendance rather than by a growth in inner healing. The underlying pain and problems people bring when they come to faith are not addressed. As a consequence, the minutiae of church organization and administration – overlaying the innermost and greatest needs of the baptized membership – assume too great an importance, occupying a disproportionate amount of attention and time.

As a congregation is eager to add to its number, the fundamental need for personal appraisal and development can be overlooked. What family, though, does not value the personal development of its members beyond corporate affirmations of confession and faith that keep people in line? More specifically, the Christian family ceases to be different from any other group, club or society when it fails to address the need for the personal and spiritual development of the individual in Christ. The newcomer looking for inner peace is overcome by an agenda of activism because he or she is led to believe that here is the relevance by which the gospel can be marketed to the world. It should come as no surprise, therefore, if the convert experiences a deep-seated sense of failure which he or she dare not admit to others in addition to the pain that is already borne from the past.

As a result we can feel that God has failed to make any real difference to our lives. The 'peace beyond understanding' appears to be completely unattainable. We settle for the spiritual second best of overlaying our failures with a general feeling that God does still care, doesn't he? As a consequence, we become even more involved in good works while failing to understand that the distinctive nature of the life the Christian can offer to the world is the incarnate, crucified and risen Christ within. That is, within the individual and within the cosmos.

The second example is also related to the hurt that a Christian community can inflict upon itself. The gospel calls for the followers of Christ to become personally vulnerable, to a deep awareness and knowledge of themselves, and to be open with one another so that love can grow and develop. But vulnerability comes with a cost that many find unacceptable.

There is, for example, the willingness of the priest to 'be there' for others when they are in greatest need. The front doorbell or the telephone can at any time and without warning signal a demand for immediate attention and help. While the image of the priest as healer responding to such real need is attractive, the reality is that this very special and important part of ministry can create serious problems for the giver. Quality family time – perhaps looked forward to in a week full of pressure from the parish – can suddenly be lost because of an emergency call-out.

The image of a 'sacrificial priesthood' also has to be applied with great care. Frustrated by the schemes and neuroses of others from building the kingdom in the parish within six days, we seriously wonder sometimes whether we are dying for the right people. There are those for whom one is more than ready to suffer in order to bring the love of God to them. There are others whom we perceive as abusing us and misusing the church for their own purposes. It is very hard to continue in the service of this second group as the calling to serve has to be balanced by the desire to confront. We forget, however, that we are meant to die even for those whom we self-righteously regard as hypocrites. At the same time we ignore our own pretence at genuine discipleship. If the life of the priest is truly subject to God then the timing of the sacrifice and the one who brings it about will be right, regardless of what we might think at the time. We cannot choose to be sacrificed only by kind and reasonable people whom we like! Sadly, though, it does not take much to divert us from the pursuit of unconditional love.

Pain can also be experienced when those for whom the priest has made sometimes considerable sacrifices turn around and reject him or her. Having voluntarily become vulnerable – and in turn having perhaps also made those closest to oneself vulnerable – subsequent rejection can produce a hard-bitten attitude that comes from the need for self-preservation as much as anything else. As a result, the vulnerability of the cross can be

exchanged for the formality of the business agenda because the
pain involved in the former is too great.

Whatever the reason, the shift between pursuing a vocation
and doing a job of work is reflected in a change in the nature of
the relationship the priest has with God.

Having a vocation or doing a job of work

In the vocation, God exists not only within and around but also
above and beyond, without limit in the love he offers and calls
forth. We follow him – often we know not where – and as we
take on the pain of others, Christ is born in us that we might be
witnesses and vehicles of true healing. From this incarnation we
are able to offer the kingdom of God to the world.

In a job of work, the God who is within becomes restricted
by a theological description governed by the necessity of human
need rather than by the soul itself (cf. Hilton, in Park, 1998).
We retain love for the like-minded, administering healing in
such a way as to be largely external to the healer. Concerns
about good housing and comfortable environment take precedence over obedience to follow wherever the Spirit leads.
Having fashioned him in the image of our own agenda, this
God becomes too small and too predictable to make any real
difference to anyone.

Yet the God who is found at the centre of our being as our
prayers descend from the head to the heart cannot be confined
by human demands. When God is described as inhabiting the
human heart, the inference is not that he can be transported
object-like within a person and lifted out and referred to and
defined as required. It is unhelpful to suggest that the majority
of people live at a distance from God while for a selected few he
is present 'inside' themselves almost as an object of their own
desires. While subjectivity and objectivity can be interchange-
able in a relationship of love, this should not lead to a distortion
of love to such a degree that God is regarded as an object in the

achievement of the desires, agendas and ambitions of the human race.

While we have to make the interior journey in order ultimately to find ourselves and discover God, it should be remembered that the soul is not confined to some small area of physical space and time which we can call 'myself'. Moreover, the God within is not similarly bound. Instead, he is the lover who is experienced and known within and above and beyond.

While God can become known at a level that is deep within the self and incarnate in life through the presence of the indwelling Christ, the existence of his love is neither restricted by human knowledge nor by humanity's willingness to receive it. The love that brought the world into being is broader, deeper and higher than we can ever conceive. God as the source of all authentic love knows the full potential of human love. While we tread the path of self-discovery, his Spirit constantly urges us on to reach new levels of love. For in direct proportion to the degree humanity grows in love, it grows also in self-knowledge. So as Christians are called to work with God in the task of ongoing creation, they cannot afford to be content with what is safe, undemanding or governed by either the needs of the institution or society.

There is no need to fear such a degree of discipleship. God does not manipulate us to love him so that we can be moved around the chessboard of human evolution. Rather than being monarchical in an autocratic manner, he invites us to explore his love and life and to find a home in them where we might truly find and be ourselves.

In this sense, God is not only with us but also ahead of us – alongside on the journey but also beyond the next horizon in even more beauty and power than at present. He is both the present that we enjoy and the future that awaits us (which might not always be the future that we choose). He brings meaning to the 'now', but even greater possibilities of fulfilment to the future.

To worship the God who is contained by our worldly plans and ambitions at the expense of the God who beckons from beyond is to reduce him to that level where his disciples can excuse their hijacking of the Holy Spirit for their own ends. To settle for the security of 'doing the job' and the pursuit of self-orientated agendas is also to settle for second best, and usually for far longer than did James and John.

Managing a vocation

To manage a vocation, on the other hand, is to be grounded in prayer as the principal way by which we align ourselves to the will of the Spirit. Such 'management' will have at least three components: trust, discernment and the willingness to move and be moved.

TRUST

The Spirit imbues the world with divine life and potential, giving its physical properties intrinsic worth and meaning. At the same time, the life of the Spirit also reveals that in the end there is very little that is worth worrying about and that reality is ultimately to be found outside the practicalities of day-to-day existence.

In light of this, the parish priest somehow has to find a way of doing justice to both the permanent and transitory aspects of his or her ministry. In order to communicate the gospel effectively to others, the priest engages with the structures of social, economic and political organizations without necessarily adopting their methods and outlook.

To pray daily 'Thy will be done on earth as it is in heaven' is to place oneself, as Archbishop Michael Ramsey suggests, on the 'Godward side of human situations' in spiritual endeavour, avoiding the more straightforward option of what might be called 'shallow secularised activism' (Ramsey, 1972).

To pursue the purposes of the Spirit for the journey is to give each day and every decision into the hands of God. While surrounded by a pace of life that tends to dehumanize people by its seemingly relentless demands, the priest especially has to maintain that inner stillness of Spirit where the voice of God can be heard.

In order to remain on this 'Godward side', we need to commit to him every action and decision before we undertake them. We cannot insert God into life in retrospect as a way of self-justification for what we might later realize was a programme of action initiated purely by ourselves. For trust involves seeking the will of God in all things and always putting his kingdom first.

In accepting a post in the parochial ministry, the only criterion that counts is whether or not we understand a particular move to be the will of God for our life and ministry. Such considerations as housing, environment and amenities are secondary. While this may sound harsh to many, vocation involves being sufficiently open so that we might go where the Spirit calls us to be. Ultimately, it is the guide who knows not only the way but also the destination of the journey. To trust so completely can be both frightening and also exciting as we discover God's plans for our lives from day to day.

Maintaining such a level of trust demands immense spiritual stamina. It is easy to slide into providing for our own safety and security in such a way that our plans leave no room for the guidance of the Spirit. When we do this, we rapidly become institutionalized both to the maintenance of the institution as an end in itself and also to our own fears and fantasies.

We may protest that it would be irresponsible not to look after ourselves and our families. Yet there is no reason why such a desire need take us away from the 'Godward side' if it is always preceded and pursued to its legitimate end by a desire to seek first the kingdom.

Trust such as this calls for much faith and prayer, particularly where the needs of family are concerned. Such prayers of sacrificial commitment, however, rarely go unanswered, frequently providing those instances when God is seen to work in the most unexpected and powerful ways.

DISCERNMENT

In order to pursue this kind of discipleship, we have to learn what it means to let go. This involves discerning what it is we like to hold on to and how we can reduce our need of it.

We may, for example, have been brought up in such a manner that our identity and the ability to be at peace with ourselves come from our relationships with others, rather than primarily from a balanced degree of self-acceptance.

Our education and the desire of well-intentioned parents may well have inculcated in us the need to be a success at work and in society, this being measured by size of income and social status. As a result, we are encouraged from an early age to express our identity in terms of income and lifestyle. Hence, one of the debilitating aspects of unemployment or serious ill-health is a feeling of a lack of self-worth. To fall off this roundabout of false self-imaging, able only to watch the progress of others from a distance, can lead to great depths of self-doubt and depression.

A vocation to the priesthood involves both a deeper awareness and involvement in the expectations of society and a withdrawal from the false forms of identity and worth it often conveys. In this context, unless we have discerned how success-orientated we are and why, together with an understanding of who it is that confers identity, we can end up using the wrong criteria to measure the effectiveness of our ministry. This can lead to false thoughts about the irrelevance of our ministry and our own form of spiritual self-doubt and depression.

In order to cherish and nurture our vocation, our prime concern is to do with the pursuit of the processes of authentic love. As part of this, we learn to love ourselves as God loves us, relinquishing the precarious options of affirmation by humanity. Moreover, it is precisely because we have put our trust in God and are following his call that *ipso facto* our lives have meaning and purpose, regardless of what society might say.

Discernment about identity will lead us to trust others more completely. Only when we have faith in ourselves can we also have faith in others. Should we fail to discern the false gods within, we will have little insight or ability to help others do the same.

THE WILLINGNESS TO MOVE AND BE MOVED

Finally, managing a vocation means that we have to be prepared to leave home every now and again in obedience to the guidance of the Spirit.

There are those who are called to remain in one place longer than others. In times past, it was more common for clergy to become imbedded in a community over several decades. Nowadays we tend to be more mobile. To stay in one place for a shorter time is not best described as 'passing through', for inevitably a parish priest is deeply involved at the heart of a community by the nature of his or her ministry. In this setting, friendships are forged and roots are put down. This is always an enormous privilege as strangers rapidly become friends, taking us to their hearts as we take them to ours. While knowing that the time will probably come for us to move on, for the time being we become real to others by taking their lives seriously, identifying with them in Christ as best we can. However, we cannot afford to make a home indefinitely with one community unless of course this is in obedience to the Spirit, for fear that we may frustrate the fulfilment of our ministry.

The vocation of a priest involves balancing many partnerships. In co-operation with God, he or she has to be prepared to move to new challenges. The mental agility required for this militates against ignoring the authority of God to make disciples of all nations, in favour of becoming leaders of a pilgrim people that has opted for the safety of a sedentary spirituality. Inevitably, there is a strange juxtaposition between deep spiritual peace and inner restlessness in the life of a spiritual leader. On the one hand there is the need to look after and build up the physical infrastructure of a worshipping community. On the other hand there is the knowledge that all such things are transitory and that covenantal love depends not upon the quality of masonry and meetings but ultimately upon the nature and depth of our relationships with each other and with God.

There is a sense in which the parish priest as leader of a pilgrim people is always on the move. Called not to stay and be still necessarily where we find life the most comfortable, we are challenged and in turn are called to confront others. Change is integral to life, and Christians need to be open and prepared to change and be changed so that they may be drawn ever closer to God and witness effectively to the world. Devoted as we may be to tradition and the sacred places we have inherited, we know that the nature of our covenantal relationship with God demands that we are constantly aware of the need to move away from anything that enslaves us. The priest can be applauded when he or she is perceived as having led others to a new and exciting ministry. The same person can also be the object of resentment and bitterness for daring to suggest that the way to Jerusalem has become obscured, even forgotten.

The spiritual and mental energy required to cope with these tensions can be very taxing, particularly when others have invested so much security in keeping things as they have always been. Yet the Spirit rarely, if ever, leaves us as we are. Moving ceaselessly over and through the waters of creation, he constantly challenges us to move on in order to further the cause of covenantal love.

There is a way, therefore, by which we can retain our idealism and enthusiasm and not settle for second best. For in the context of our acknowledgement of the pre-eminence of God we are to seek his will in all things. Yet, avoiding the sin of pride is not so much achieved by constant reappraisal of our approach to ministry as by the effect of our life of prayer. As we become increasingly immersed in the life of prayer – both heartbeat and other forms, informal and formal – we become incorporated into the life of God almost without realizing it. His life and ours merge increasingly and almost imperceptibly to the extent that the line where one ends and the other begins becomes increasingly difficult to draw. From such a conjunction the idolatrous desire to rule the world is revealed for what it is, this temptation being but the sign that our prayer life comes from a dysfunctional and demonic background. As Christ refused it himself in the wilderness and to the two brothers on the road, so are we to refuse it today. For strength is found not in the merging of two powers but in the union of Lover and beloved. To this we shall return in the next chapter.

In a loving relationship between two human beings, as we have seen, there is a voluntary surrender of some freedom but not of individuality. In fact, the unconditional love that they share helps them to achieve their potential as individuals through a process of constant breaking down and building up. This affects the soul in a sacramental way as salvation is centred on the fulfilment of one's potential in love and the achievement of the purposes of God for ourselves and others. But where the love of one usurps the freedom and individuality of another, it becomes destructive and personal fulfilment a fantasy not only for the one who is abusing the relationship, but also for the one who is being abused.

The one who prays earnestly, 'loses' himself or herself in God by voluntary self-surrender, so that in balanced harmony of relationship with him a new life – authentic life – comes into being. In *The Way of Silent Love*, a Carthusian has written, 'One must become God to know God,' and so by prayer a new identity is discovered and the believer is led ever deeper into the mystery of the being of God where detailed description is impossible. This process is described in the words of John the

Baptist: 'He must increase, but I must decrease.' For, 'True inner prayer is to stop talking and to listen to the wordless voice of God within our heart; it is to cease doing things on our own, and to enter into the action of God' (Bishop Kallistos Ware, 1974).

This is central to our life with God. Through much prayer, the self becomes lost in him. But not lost in the sense of being destroyed or even belittled. Quite the contrary. The individuality of our life that is composed of our likes and dislikes, ambitions, agendas, careers and conformity, the need for that acclamation which is conferred by society and aimed at self-preservation, is done away with as the new person emerges. As our prayers take us deeper, we become increasingly less aware of ourselves and our worldly needs and more aware of ourselves and our eternal, spiritual identity.

To pray in this way is to accept that God is in charge of the life and ministry of the priest, not in a detached and authoritarian way but in the balanced mutual service of love.

This – and so much else – is true not only for the priest but for all those who feel called to spiritual leadership and also for the priesthood of all believers.

Devoid of individual plans and ambitions, the priest comes to know that he or she is both nothing and everything, nobody and everybody. Created out of nothing, the inner self is drawn into the life of God, where we find that we are whole only when we are one with him without any attempt to achieve equal status. In this world spiritual leaders are nothing other than that which other human beings allow them to be, whereas in this life (and the next life as the two merge into one) he or she is nothing other than that which God gives.

This is summed up for us in the prayer at the consummation of the Holy Eucharist in the Divine Liturgy of St John Chrysostom:

Thou didst bring us into being out of nothing, and when we had fallen away didst raise us up again, and didst not cease to do all things until Thou hadst brought us back to heaven, and hast endowed us with Thy kingdom which is to come. For all these things we give thanks to Thee, and to Thy Only-begotten Son, and Thy Holy Spirit.

NOTES

1 Susan Marginelli, a housewife in New England, talking about alternative living styles as quoted in the *National Geographic Magazine*.

REFERENCES

A Carthusian, *The Way of Silent Love*, Darton, Longman and Todd, London, 1993, p. 70.

Bishop Kallistos Ware, *The Power of the Name*, Marshall, Morgan and Scott, London (© The Sisters of the Love of God), 1974, p. 8.

T. Park, *The English Mystics*, SPCK, London, 1998, p. 47.

M. Ramsey, *The Christian Priest Today*, SPCK, London, 1972, p. 17.

3

THE PRAYER OF THE DYING SEED

'You do not know what you are asking.'

(Mark 10.38)

I seriously doubt that it would be possible to devise an ordination training course which would prepare candidates completely – or even adequately – for spiritual leadership in general and for the life of the parish priest in particular.

The fact that so many priests survive – and by no means all do – is due at least in part to their great faith and the abundance of the mercy of God, not to mention the ability to think on one's feet and compromise!

At ordination, can deacons ever dream of the pressures to which they will be subjected later on? Ever realize how many times their hearts will break as they stand alongside others in the most trying of life's crises? Ever anticipate how much their work at times will leave them emotionally and spiritually drained?

The prophet Jeremiah seems almost to speak on our behalf:

O Lord, you have enticed me,
    and I was enticed;
you have overpowered me,
    and you have prevailed.
I have become a laughing stock all day long;
    everyone mocks me ...
If I say, 'I will not mention him,
    or speak any more in his name,'

34

then within me there is something like a burning fire
  shut up in my bones;
I am weary with holding it in,
  and I cannot.

(Jeremiah 20.7, 9)

As we saw in the previous chapter, when the initial enthusiasm has worn off and the fire of love is burning low, we too can feel caught between the inner drive of our vocation that refuses to let us go and the outer longing to give up, run away and settle for a more peaceful life. Not infrequently Christian ministers have to confront feelings of failure as they tend to assume that they should be stronger than they are.

The words above of Jesus to James and John may be a source of encouragement when things are not going according to plan. Sometimes, despite our best efforts, we feel it only fair to expect certain outcomes as a result of our dedication to God and our ministry. Here, though, we are cautioned against any assumption that might define our discipleship in any predictable way. Not only are we to place our present and future into the hands of God but also the way in which covenantal love can best achieve its aims.

This kind of love invariably operates contrary to our instincts. The usual mechanics of cause and effect are replaced by values that we find well-nigh impossible to manufacture ourselves. So it is that by the Spirit we are able to move from a position of self-preservation to self-sacrifice. In common with James and John, the priest has no idea what he or she is asking, not simply because we, too, ask from the wrong motives but because we also frequently confuse goodness with Godliness.

Goodness can be established by the implementation of laws that govern human conduct and which inevitably divide society into a hierarchical structure. It is often thought that this system differentiates between the good and the bad whereas in reality it principally separates the parties that are involved with administering the law from the rest. Hence the bias of the Divine to the weak and oppressed. Not because they are more worthy of love than the rich and powerful but because, while they are just as sinful, they make no pretence at being superior to others. A parish priest can operate within such a hierarchical structure and pursue goodness which will mean that the church he or she serves will – in all probability – be no different from any other human institution with similar aims concerning justice and social integration.

Godliness, on the other hand, creates an egalitarian society where no one is considered better than anyone else. Identity is conferred by grace equally to all those who live within the love of God. Here personal ambition and the desire to control others are absent, as the Spirit of love binds together all the members of the family in mutual love and service.

Here the parish priest can dispense with any system that does not release the gifts and vision of others for the kingdom and embrace the untidiness and unpredictability of unconditional love. This church will be a witness to the love of Christ, and from it the world will come to know the meaning of a God who longs to be incarnate in the lives and loves of all his people.

So it is, in common with the disciples, that we have to learn not to be content with that kind of ministry to others that has our own well-being as its prime concern. Instead, we pray for help that we might be able to place ourselves at the disposal of others. For it is at the foot of the cross that we can discover and offer to them the true freedom of love. Moving from a position of power to dependence, however, is difficult and costly as we shall see.

Working from weakness

The perception that we should be strong in our service of Christ can reveal much about our inability to accept our own weaknesses. In addition, it shows a misapprehension of the way God gives life. Strength in perseverance and faith are much needed qualities of the Christian leader. But a priest who feels he or she should themselves be powerful to build up the Body of Christ is one who can quickly disarm and deskill those with whom they have been called to work. The priest cannot pretend to hold a monopoly on knowing Christ. Rather, he or she strives to enable Christ to become a reality in the lives of those he or she seeks to serve. This does not mean having all the answers to all the questions all the time! Instead, the spiritual leader is committed to patient, sensitive listening so that the voice of God may be heard and love revealed in all circumstances. This will involve from time to time having to admit that we do not know the answer to a particular problem while remaining committed to helping others seek and find Christ. In so doing, we can discover the way to deal with it.

When we read of how Jesus exhorted his followers to be perfect as their heavenly Father is perfect (Matthew 5.48), we are not to mistranslate the word *teleios* to mean 'without fault'. As a result of this misunderstanding many Christian leaders have set an impossible standard of human infallibility for others while never achieving it themselves. By contrast, the meaning of this Greek word has more to do with our understanding of the purpose for which God has put us into this world and the fulfilment of our potential in the pursuit of this.

Perfection, in this context, is therefore about that place where the life of God emerges – often painfully slowly – through the frailty of our human condition. In his book *Open to Judgement*, Rowan Williams tells us: 'A human being is holy not because he or she triumphs by will-power over chaos and guilt and leads a flawless life, but because that life shows the victory of God's faithfulness *in the midst* of disorder and imperfection' (Williams, 1994).

The spiritual leader who finds it hard to accept his or her imperfection clearly has much to learn about the grace of God. For God not only makes up for our shortcomings, he also uses them creatively for his purposes. So-called perfect people and perfect schemes rarely, if ever, have God as the source of their inspiration or energy. Though we think God calls us to our strength, invariably his call is to our weakness.

Unless those who are involved in spiritual leadership have this realistic understanding of themselves, they are unlikely to appreciate what it is that God wants to give through them. Even the most dedicated of people can give in to unnecessary frustration because they become disillusioned with their own efforts to lead a Christian life. Brother Lawrence (1978) said: 'For the first ten years I suffered much. The apprehension that I was not devoted to God as I wished to be, my past sins always present to my mind, and the great unmerited favours which God did me, were the matter and source of my sufferings.' He found, however, that by letting go of his self-criticism and concentrating instead on having simple faith, humility and love, he was able to receive an inner peace and contentment as he strove to lead his life in the presence of God.

Sadly, we tend not to be good at this kind of letting go. Our natural drives encourage us to hang on to any tool that enhances our chances of survival. This is just as true of spiritual as it is of physical resources. The rigours of ministry often cause the leader to become isolated, even withdrawn. Parish priests sometimes take great pride in their self-sufficiency without realizing that from this position they cannot live with or serve the people of God. Holding on to what might be perceived as their personal strength, however, usually means holding out on those who long to know the love of God.

Being broken

Over the years God takes the life of the priest – as he will anyone who decides to leave home to follow him – and bit by bit breaks and rebuilds it countless times until the false layer of pride and reliance upon human strength have been broken down. What is left is still an unworthy vessel but now at least one which can be used powerfully for the sake of the kingdom. For, having found its place in God's scheme of things, it can fulfil its role as it is led and empowered by the Spirit of love.

This is not to say that a person cannot resist this process of transformation – or sanctification – either by stubbornly refusing to admit that he or she can be broken or by rejecting the goodness that comes from brokenness.

The archetypal story of Jacob wrestling with God at Peniel (Genesis 32.22–32) has become a common experience in the lives of many who long to serve God, in whatever capacity. The way in which God brings us to the point of dependence on him usually takes place over a number of years as it did in the life of Jacob. We happily continue to run our own lives ignoring his pleas to walk with him, until according to his will and timing we are made to realize – usually through some pain that threatens to cripple us – how far away from him we really are and how much we need him in order to live.

Yet, refusing to let go, we wrestle with God for the control of our lives and ministry. All he wants to do is to fill us with the life of his Spirit and allow us to swim in the sea of his love. We can be terrified, though, of surrendering our lives to him for fear that the self we have engineered and have come to trust and accept will be drowned. We prefer to have the freedom to decide for ourselves the best way to serve God.

Sooner or later this fake façade of discipleship cracks under the strain and we are left unable to manage under our own devices in quite the same way as before. We are humbled to the extent that we begin to see ourselves again in others. This time, though, we see the weak rather than the strong aspects of our personalities. Points of contact emerge that we never knew were there before. Instead of seeing ourselves as the principal source of spiritual life in a community, we realize that our leadership is dependent upon the spirituality of others. We realize, too, that we are constantly in need of Christ's healing touch which often depends upon our relationship with those to whom we seek to minister. We find that we need God's love and healing through them as much as they need these through us. Thus, in bearing one another's burdens, we fulfil the law of Christ (Galatians 6.2). Spiritual leadership then is a model of collaborative ministry where service of the other is the norm, where no one makes pretence at being stronger or better or more learned or more spiritually minded than anyone else. These are attributes of discipleship and leadership that may only be conferred upon the priest by others. The priest has many roles, but they can only be given by God to the one who knows how much he or she needs to lean on others so that the life of God can become real in them.

Hence the most significant words in the gospel record for a personal understanding of the cost of Christian ministry are those spoken by Jesus to his disciples in Jerusalem before his arrest and betrayal: 'Very truly, I tell you, unless a grain of wheat falls into the earth and dies, it remains just a single grain; but if it dies, it bears much fruit' (John 12.24). This might have been a direct reference to the burial of Christ in the tomb followed by his resurrection on the third day. Alternatively, it might simply be a paradigm relating to the need for the Christian disciple to be prepared to die to self before finding new life in the kingdom. Either way, reading it today the priest – as anyone who wishes to make Christ known to others – is warned to be prepared to die and rise with Christ if his or her life is to be an effective witness to the truth of healing love. Archbishop Michael Ramsey (1972) once wrote of the immature minister: 'He may be liked and admired, but he will not become a true priest until his heart is broken.'

If a Christian minister refuses to be broken, how else will he or she be opened up and the life within given to the world? The alternative is to remain behind our barriers of false respectability from where good works and *bons mots* can be dispensed with little if any real cost to ourselves. It is only when we have been taken from our position of safety, and have experienced the freezing temperatures of the spiritual chill of our times, that we can begin to realize that it is only here, as the life of God thrusts upwards and outwards relentlessly from within, that authentic, sacrificial love comes to the surface. What is more, we have to be prepared to experience this through as many winters as God deems it will take for the eventual harvest to be as plentiful as possible.

In view of this, it is a sobering thought that those without a faith experience these winters devoid of the hope of spring. They rely upon human goodness, and no more, to get them through their homelessness, their grief, their feelings of rejection, separation from loved ones, inadequacies in relationships, their fears and self-doubt and so on. How pertinent, then, that the Christian minister too should be made to experience something of their darkness. And what penitence should be ours when we complain about our cross despite our knowledge of resurrection!

Giving in to God for life

The Spirit challenges the world of self-sufficiency with the kingdom of self-sacrifice. As it is common for those entering the church to wear their survival paraphernalia unchallenged, the result is a pollution of the church and a spiritual fall-out that damages, if not completely halts, the progress of covenantal love. While it tends to be an unwelcome and painful process – and we avoid it wherever possible – when we give in, such worldly clothing is taken from us that we might put on Jesus Christ. Coming to terms with the less than desirable aspects of our inner selves can be very demanding, yet it is of fundamental importance to do this, as it is from within that the Spirit energizes us to give life to others. The streams of living water flow out from the heart of a person; if that heart is impure, so too will be the water of life. Help with this comes either directly through those closest to us, who often know us better than we do ourselves, or through our enemies who more often than not are the most perceptive about our weaknesses. Self-knowledge can also come when, through unwelcome circumstances visited on us, we are made to confront not the person we like to project, but the person we really are.

We who would call ourselves the children of God, while accepting and enjoying the privileges of his Fatherhood, have also to accept his guidance and discipline not as something that is destructive – although it will feel like this at times – but as a sign of his love for us and for the person he wants us to become: ' "My child, do not regard lightly the discipline of the Lord, or lose heart when you are punished by him; for the Lord disciplines those whom he loves, and chastises every child whom he accepts" ' (Hebrews 12.5–6).

This means that we have to surrender everything in the cause of the gospel. There is no room for lukewarm half measures or tepid discipleship. The vulnerability of the priest has to include a willingness to stand before God and humanity, damaged and divested of the earthly trappings of this life and the concerns of this world, yet still prepared to risk all in loving obedience of the one whose constant commitment to us is most clear when we are least committed to our personal agendas. We may find that we feel that God cannot break us any more than he has already until he does so again, this time perhaps taking away even that which we most cherish. When this happens, we realize, as our lives are reduced once again to rubble, that we still have not ceased to wrestle with God. As we claw our way back once again from nothing, we find ourselves purged further still, weaker than ever, yet stronger, in greater need of the company and love of God and others, and therefore even more able than ever before to hold together his life and theirs. Truly, once the hand has been set to the plough there is no looking back.

This breaking process, therefore, is not – as it might seem at times – the way to defeat and death. On the contrary, it is the way to life. Perhaps this is why, despite all that the spiritual leader is called to face, there remains a willingness to be driven on from within.

James and John were driven, and they too were to be purified in the service of Christ. They could not have known the full implications of their question. Their enthusiasm at this time was not matched by a realistic awareness of what lay ahead, how they were to be broken and remade in a new Christ-like image of God.

If this breaking process is the way to life then we need not fear it. Instead, we can welcome it, embrace it and find within it not a cause of sorrow but of joy.

This holiness is to be found not in the prayer of one who prays from a position of perceived strength but in the prayer of one who, having been broken, is committed to the continual process of returning. For it is in returning – particularly from a disaster that has all but destroyed us – that we find renewed and deeper companionship with the Father who runs to meet us and throws a feast in our honour.

Similarly, in the service of others it is not in faultlessness but in being completely committed to the continual process of 'trying, dying and rising' that the priest – and anyone else for that matter who wishes to serve Christ – becomes holy. Devout disciples try hard to serve their masters and their fellow human beings, but frequently find themselves not on their feet but flat on their faces. From here with the help of God they have to stand up again and carry on, not in self-recrimination for having made a mess of things, but in a greater knowledge of the nature of our servanthood. The spiritual leader who refuses to admit he or she falls regularly, or who gives up trying altogether, will not of course bear these marks of holiness which – as we have seen – can only be attributed by others and witnessed ultimately by God in his Spirit in us.

As the priest becomes incorporated into the being of God so

the continual process of being broken and remade, of death and resurrection, becomes intrinsic to the life of prayer. And herein lies real strength:

> This is how God will judge us all. Not by what we have achieved; not by some man-made measure of success, but by how best we have tried ... Believe me, the whole of the spiritual life, the very essence of mystical prayer is about Dying through Trying. It is not the coward; it is the saint who dies a thousand times before his death and it is in his Dying, through his Trying that he reaches the height of the spiritual life; total identity, complete at-onement with the Christ of Easter Day.
>
> (Torkington, 1987)

This message is most clearly spelt out by St Paul whose life and ministry were hampered – so he thought to begin with – by a painful physical ailment, an ailment he refers to as his 'thorn in the flesh'. His words are familiar to all who have found themselves in similar situations where the apparent senseless-ness of pain seems to contradict the will of God who urgently seeks disciples in every generation to serve him:

> Three times I appealed to the Lord about this, that it would leave me, but he said to me, 'My grace is sufficient for you, for power is made perfect in weakness.' So I will boast all the more gladly of my weaknesses, so that the power of Christ may dwell in me. Therefore I am content with weaknesses, insults, hardships, persecutions, and calamities for the sake of Christ; for whenever I am weak, then I am strong.
>
> (2 Corinthians 12.8–10)

God does not give as the world gives, so we are prepared by him to receive the most precious gift of all by becoming open in our frailty.

The Dark Night

The prayer of the dying seed is the one we utter when we encounter the darkest and coldest moments of our lives. But as with all the gifts of God's love we can resist these altogether. In writing that it had to die in order to bear fruit, John knew that the seed could remain but a seed if it so wished, although it would never fulfil its destiny for life. In this sense we only die to the degree that we permit the purgation of our souls, by accepting the seemingly endless trials by which God seeks to make us part of himself. At these times little makes sense, God seems far away and we can feel shorn of everything we ever held dear and thought to be of importance. There is little meaning to be found in our suffering at the time. It gnaws deep into us and we are left experiencing something of what St John of the Cross described as the Dark Night of the Soul. Having given our lives to God we experience a loss of conventional life – partly as a result of our own decisions and partly because of the discipline of God – that makes us in a way almost strangers to those who have not encountered the same experience.

More than this, in the darkness of this night, there is even a degree of the 'dissolution of the self' if we permit it to take place. It is itself a terrifying ordeal. For it is at this point that we lose all the familiar points that give identity to ourselves and to God. We do not bring this suffering on ourselves, nor is it the kind of suffering that comes from evil or the life of a fallen world. Instead it comes from God and we are helpless in its grip. We are wrestled to the ground – what is left of us, that is – and at this point we fear that we have all but ceased to be.

The prayer of the dying seed is one that is beyond thoughts and words. It is a cry both of fear and also of adoration. It is the love that does not even need conscious expression for it is performed by the Spirit deep within the human spirit. As a form of prayer it is extreme in the heat of its intensity in comparison with the coldness of its environment. Extreme because of our inability to experience it in any conventional way. Extreme given the lack of control we have over it, for its purity is uncontaminated by those emotions, images, thoughts and expressions with which we tend in more normal times to overlay our prayers. For in that we feel we have died, we are incapable of contaminating the union that at this time is achieved between the Holy Spirit and our spirit. In this darkness and godlessness is to be found a unique union with God that depends solely upon his grace and action within us. Of ourselves we can do nothing to enhance this process. Yet when the darkness disappears we discover the most wonderful and life-giving truth of all: namely, that we have been raised to our feet and now stand with God in a new life as he becomes born in us and we in him. In short, we discover our eternal selves.

During such a time of darkness which usually happens only once in a lifetime – and during the many other lesser nights when we have been broken and God seems far away and the spiritual life remote – we can find a valid way of prayer through performing simple spiritual exercises. The very act of lighting a candle and standing by it in silence is a prayer in itself. So, too, the act of standing before an icon or simply kneeling before a cross. Or just holding on to a prayer rope or rosary. There is no need for words – they are irrelevant and largely meaningless at this time – as we rely completely upon God to work through our pain in love, drawing us ever closer to himself. We are tempted to think that we are not praying, that we are wasting our time and that God is not active at this point. Yet rather than being our most pathetic attempts at prayer, they are quite possibly our most effective, as we rely completely upon the grace of God. For since our bodies are the temple in which he has chosen to dwell, our every breath has immense sacramental significance. If only we knew it.

We are to welcome darkness as the precursor of new life and service, as a time of further release from those things that have tied us down. For it is in keeping faith in the darkest night and in lesser darknesses that we are most likely to become the people God has called us to be. After all, it has been a principle of life from the beginning that the Light of God's Word shines most clearly in the darkness of the world and the human condition. It was, indeed, in the darkness that followed the death of Jesus that the dead were set free.

REFERENCES

Brother Lawrence, *The Practice of the Presence of God*, Spire Books, London, 1978, pp. 34–5.

M. Ramsey, *The Christian Priest Today*, SPCK, London, 1972, p. 90.

D. Torkington, *Peter Calvay – Prophet*, Spennithorne Publications, Liverpool, 1987.

R. Williams, *Open to Judgement*, Darton, Longman and Todd, London, 1994, p. 136.

4

The Prayer of Intercession

'Are you able to drink the cup that I drink?'

(Mark 10.38)

While James and John thought they understood them, it is unclear from the gospel text what precisely Jesus meant by these words. However, we will take it that this question refers to the cup of discipleship which God gives to those he calls to minister in his name (Mark 14.36). This saying, which comes from a time when Jesus was foretelling his death and resurrection, followed by his prayer in the Garden of Gethsemane concerning the cup of suffering,[1] suggests that those who would follow him are called to seek out and embrace the suffering of the world. For it is only through this kind of sacrificial love that the pain of the world can be redeemed. Such an approach is radically different from the way humanity tends to behave.

Genuine altruistic behaviour can be hard to find. People naturally prefer security to sacrifice. When loving one's neighbour is perceived as being rewarded with continued personal existence after death, such charity can quickly be infused with motives that are at best selfish. Genuine love can be found in the desire to help close family and friends who are in need. Even in these instances, though, it is often remarkable how short the patience of the one who gives can become when his or her own security is threatened. On a larger scale, in a world that is becoming smaller as a result of the revolution in communications technology, there are signs of genuine sympathy to the pain of others who live in faraway places – caused perhaps by a natural disaster or despotic political leadership – on purely humanitarian grounds. Although, there is a suspicion here that it is easier to appear altruistic in one's care of others when they live at a distance and do not impinge on one's own sovereign territory and resources.

The incarnation, however, makes authentic altruistic behaviour possible by its promotion of a common spiritual identity where one person finds fulfilment in the triumph of healing love over the pain of another. The Church is called to make this love incarnate in the life of humanity by the work of the Spirit of Christ in and through its members. By definition, therefore, it exists not to produce an eternal life insurance policy for its members, but to participate with God in the task of bringing light to the areas of creation where darkness remains.

While most people would prefer not to permit the problems of others to jeopardize their own safety, the security they seek for themselves is itself often elusive. Almost as soon as a lifestyle is established, it can be dismantled by any number of unforeseen circumstances: health problems, redundancy, relationship breakdown, political instability and so on.

On the other hand, security for the Christian is found in an active co-operation in the process of the healing of humanity. Carried out as part of the ongoing covenant of love between God and humanity, this life alone can grant long-term stability to the world and the establishment of justice and peace.

Embracing the suffering of the world

To seek out and embrace the suffering of the world has no enhanced survival implications for the healer, arising as it does from a love that has already rendered such reward-seeking meaningless. In addition, this love is not an offer from some external source of aid which might give in a paternalistic manner and with conditions. Instead, it is the natural consequence of the common spiritual identity of humanity where all personalities ultimately find their fulfilment in the personality of Christ. Creation, itself energized by the dynamic presence of the Word, holds the Life of Christ, and the Church in its role as the leaven of society re-presents this truth in bread and wine. So, at the conclusion of Christian ministry, self-congratulation and self-enhancement are displaced by the knowledge that at the end of the day we have only done our duty (Luke 17.10).

The priest in particular – though by no means exclusively – is called to seek out the brokenness of the world so that its wounds might be bound up and healed. Mission in this sense is first and foremost about joining with others on their journey. It is about listening to their stories, being in dialogue with them, and bringing all that this relationship becomes into the presence of Christ. This is in stark contrast to the high-pressure selling of a belief/value system which begins with an invitation to en-forced systematic conformity rather than an offer of freedom and fullness of life in fellowship with God.

We can see from the Gospels that Jesus appears to have been about this work wherever he went. He brought the healing love of God to bear not only in the particular miracle stories that we have been given, but also in his teaching and reactions to the stories of those around him who had, for the most part, fallen foul of the religious law.

In this context, the priest has to be sure of what exactly he or she has to offer. The priest does not come to the unemployed as an expert on job creation, nor to those who are encountering difficulties in marriage as an expert in this kind of counselling, nor to those suffering problems of the mind as an expert in psychology or psychiatry. While any individual minister may have specific expertise in one or more of these areas, he or she comes primarily as one who has been called to bring the presence of the healing love of Christ to the dis-ease of others.

Mission leads inevitably, therefore, to the ministry of inter-cession in which specific prayers offered to God on behalf of others are the expression of a deeper relationship. The two have to go together. Authentic love and compassion are not accessed by someone else's sacrifice – in the physical or spiritual sense – on an altar for the appeasement of the wrath of God. Instead, they become realized in the continued sacrifice of the love of Christ in the self-giving of the one who intercedes.

The prayer of intercession has much to do with the way in which the priest moves from the security of his or her own position to be with someone who, for whatever reason, is finding the journey to be too much and is travelling in isolation from others and from God. Having joined in the journey of another, the priest remains with that person in order to hold their pain in creative tension with the healing love of God.

What is meant, though, in this instance by 'creative tension'?

Intercession as creative tension

There can be no doubt that the prayer of intercession can be hard work. The function of the one who intercedes is not to coerce another person to move to stand where he or she is: 'If you believe what I do then God will come to your aid and you will feel much better.' Or to attempt to tell God to do what we consider is best for someone else. Rather, it is to be committed to journey together, encountering the depths which threaten both, while at the same time being committed to grow towards an enhanced development of self-knowledge and a greater awareness of one's destiny.

Forming value judgements about others plays no part in intercessory prayer. Except in very extreme cases, the role of the priest is not so much to try and prevent a soul from being cast into the unquenchable fire, as to acknowledge that the fellow-traveller's pain provides the possibility for further personal development. In this sense, all intercession is about continuing spiritual growth in terms of the furtherance of a person's journey into truth and meaning which come from God. It has

51

been part of the faith of the Church from its earliest days that the life of Christ was as much – if not more – about bringing about the fulfilment of the potential for God in every human life as it was about a deliverance from judgement and eternal damnation.

In intercession it is important to learn to tell the difference between the guidance of the Spirit and the desire to rush in with our own answers. Holding others and the world in creative tension often means that the priest is called not so much to give answers as to ask questions – sometimes awkward ones. 'Are you able to drink the cup I drink?' is not simply asking James and John if they have been realistic in working out whether or not they possess what it will take to be disciples. The question also asks them to take responsibility for their journey with God and have ownership of their desires, feelings, ambitions and failures. The inability of a person to take charge of his or her life is often the cause for the perceived failure of intercessory prayer. God, however, will not do for us what we can do ourselves.

There is a sense in which we can see that Jesus was inter-ceding for James and John from the start of their conversation. First, while travelling with them he listened attentively to them not only to hear what they were saying but also to read the deeper message behind their words. Jesus then asks questions of James and John to help them own their feelings and understand exactly what it is that they are asking. By so doing, he recognizes the freedom of the individual in decision-making and the need for everyone to be responsible for their thoughts and plans. Having done this, his final response reveals the creative tension that takes place when the love of God is brought to bear on the disciples' lives even though at the time they may have misunderstood it themselves. This final stage of intercession is by far the longest. While remaining with them, Jesus allows the two brothers to work out their ambitions, questions, pain and so on in relation to whatever new setting or degree of understanding the love of God can lead them into.

The intercessory work of the parish priest or spiritual leader frequently follows this model. We have not been called to solve the problems of others but to lead them to understand their difficulties in a new light – the Light of Christ. And while we cannot physically remain with them all the time, we do so in our prayers of intercession and through our love as we continue to hold them close to God. Rarely, if ever, do we put conditions on our intercessions for the answers are usually found as people discover the love of God coming to bear on them. The answer to this kind of prayer can sometimes be found in the removal of the cause of pain but more often in a renewed appreciation of it within the love of God. While an initial respite may be experienced, it is unlikely that quick answers will be found as the primary stages of creative tension begin to work themselves out. More often, in the listening, humble questioning and support of covenantal love the priest continues to walk with those who suffer.

It is an enormous privilege to be asked to perform this ministry for others. To be asked to help someone in need provides anyone with the opportunity to achieve something of nobility in the human spirit. To be invited as a priest to enter into the life journey of another – sometimes at a very deep level with people we might not know particularly well – is to find ourselves in a position of great acceptance and trust. It is rarely a straightforward process – hence the understanding of 'creative tension' – for through pain, need and suffering, God frequently gives people the opportunity to turn their lives around and face the One from whom their backs may have been turned for some time. Whether straightforward or not, it is always a source of great blessing, providing endless moments to be valued and cherished for ever.

To a degree, this process of intercession never ceases. Once we have experienced deep fellowship with others, there is a real sense in which we remain on the journey together, even though the time of specific intercession is over. Shared experience of the journey produces a bond that is not easily broken. It is not unusual for a person to return to the same intercessor in future times of need. Moreover, humility also requires that the priest accepts that at a future date he or she may well need the prayers of the one for whom they prayed earlier on. There are few more moving experiences than this and to this we shall return.

Earlier in Mark's Gospel we are told how four people brought their friend on a stretcher to be healed by Jesus. In a similar manner, many people of prayer who are caught up in a society that allows little room for regular spiritual recreation often look to the priest to carry either themselves or their friends or loved ones into the presence of God.

Unlocking the life of Christ

This is one of the functions of the priest at the Eucharist. Here he or she is not a negotiator between demanding God and wayward people, nor a performer of magic tricks, but a facilitator of the symbols of love that unlock the life of Christ. The priest does not perform actions and say specific words dictated by God to people who are not themselves worthy enough to speak to him. Instead, he or she leads the prayer of the people who, by the operation of the Holy Spirit, themselves become the Body of Christ, the Church.

Since the death of Christ, access to God has been immediate for everyone who wants it. The picture of the curtain of the Temple torn in two is a powerful symbol that reminds us that the believer does not need to go through priest or sacrificial ritual to approach the throne of God. Nevertheless, the intercession of the priest in the Eucharist is central, in that in an inclusive way it helps the life and sacrifice of Christ to become present to the people in this sacrament.

Here Christ is revealed and received by faith in bread and wine by the sacrifice of a broken and contrite heart. The priest stands not between but alongside God and humanity in that place where he or she can offer prayer that bind others to God. By journeying in this manner, the priest can re-present the sacrifice of Christ to others so that, released from fear and worry, they might be empowered to receive and be with him. By bearing the faithful into the presence of God the priest helps them to see and receive Christ in ordinary bread and wine made extraordinary by faith, that is, our faith in God and his in us. Standing in this place of creative tension where God and humanity meet, the priest facilitates the work of the Spirit so that the Divine potential is released in creation both in suffering and celebration.

Living in this state of creative tension, the priest is to be a vehicle of the grace of God. The priest is specially equipped – though by no means exclusively – to do this because he or she has been called to concentrate on prayer and the proximity of his or her life to God. As a result, the priest can help others see how close to God they are already and then facilitate the process of their moving closer still. Intercession, by my definition, is 'prayer as it takes place within the dynamic of God's love and ours'. If the life of an intercessor is not one of prayer, the love of God will be largely absent as he or she tries to fulfil this role.

This places a tremendous responsibility upon those who have a primary calling to intercede for others. For when the priest loses touch with God, the people he or she serves will lose one of their principal points of contact. We are not referring here to the doubts that afflict us all at regular intervals nor to the arid times we have already mentioned. These, rather, are the occasions – which happen to most priests sooner or later – when prayer and the things of the spiritual life grind to a halt as a result of our own faults, forgetfulness and sinfulness. At such times the intercessor should not hesitate to ask for intercession. There is no room for false pride or spiritual arrogance, for as we 'explore the human heart this is what we shall see: the kingdom of heaven in the soul of the saint, but in the soul of the sinner are darkness and torment' (Silouan, 1975), and on any given day either condition might be found in the priest. So, if we are to cope with this form of prayer, we have to realize that those who give also need to remember how to receive. Hence the need for prayer partners or soul friends who themselves will daily raise us up in prayer for God's protection and blessing.

A spiritual leader cannot, therefore, intercede for others from the fringes of life or from the comfort that can be gleaned from ecclesiastical position. Instead, he or she is called to be engaged in the task of being as close to God as possible, thereby becoming as close to others as is required for intercession to be effective. We cannot stand by our neighbours in their times of need if we are not also standing by God while standing in the world. This brings us back to the importance of our personal times of quiet prayer and reflection.

The need to be still

It is, of course, up to each individual priest to set his or her own target. Two hours' prayer and meditation first thing in the morning are clearly not going to go down well at home if there is a spouse with needs to be met, and children to be taken to school, whose lives should not be blighted by the vocation of one of their parents. A married priest has two vocations and he or she is required to do justice to them both. What we can say, however, is that as each minister sets his or her own target, it should be one that will be demanding, albeit not unreasonably so, and should not be fitted into the day merely when there is a spare moment. Finally, the discipline arrived at – in discussion with family and friends if the office is also part of the home – needs to be sufficiently robust so that the working day is orientated around the prayer of intercession and not the other way round.

The prayer of intercession, therefore, begins not with the person for whom we are praying or working but with ourselves. In this context, to pray 'Father, into your hands I commend my

Spirit' is not selfishly to ask for protection for oneself. On the contrary, it is to ask God to watch over us and to take the sacrifice of our lives, and work his will through them for the good of others.

How we begin the day in prayer usually determines how effective our ministry of intercession will be. This was clearly apparent to the mind of an outsider observing the life of Mother Teresa of Calcutta who wrote: 'Each day Mother Teresa meets Jesus first in the Mass, whence she derives sustenance and strength; then in each needing, suffering soul she sees and tends. They are one and the same Jesus; at the altar and in the streets. Neither exists without the other' (Muggeridge, 1971).

There is a need, therefore, for the parish priest to pay close attention to the structure of each working day so that it is the Spirit who sets the agenda. When the demands of others dictate the shape of ministry, frustration and lack of spiritual fulfilment produce a special kind of stress of their own.

Wherever possible in the week, the priest should endeavour to spend up to the first two hours of the working day in prayer, Bible study and reading. The achievement of this will be more straightforward on some days and in some weeks than others, but it is nevertheless a realistic target for which to aim. There are countless reasons why this could be said to be impossible, but to try and set the day's agenda this way is to make prayer a priority as the source of life and power for ministry.

Using set forms of prayer, together with time for contemplative and meditative reflection, the priest is much more likely to recognize those for whom he or she has been called to pray. As a result, no meeting during the day becomes a haphazard occurrence. Everything becomes pregnant with possibilities for God. Every encounter with another individual, meeting with groups or even the most mundane tasks are prefaced and borne along by prayer.

There are deadlines and demands from many quarters that are to do with desk work, visiting, sermon preparation, committee work and so on. But for a priest, prayer always comes first. When it does, it is remarkable how much more straightforward the other tasks become. Levels of stress increase when we worry about things in the past and future because we have forgotten that both are in the hands of God. If we focus on the problems of the day, we can find that yesterday and tomorrow's problems often disappear.

Intercession for some is about changing systems and organizing campaigns to help others. While these are signs of love in action – and without them radical change seldom takes place – the spiritual leader will address in prayer the deep-seated causes of evil. Programmes for corporate action that take place without such spiritual undergirding are just as prone to evil distortion as the system they are trying to reform or replace. Some may be called to intercede in prayer, while others are set free by such prayer to act. Usually we are called to some degree both to pray and to act.

The cost involved

The cost of this prayer of intercession should not be under-estimated. As a Christian minister leaves the safety of his or her own territory, not always by choice but because of the request of another, they can place themselves in danger. Those whom we seek to help may not be as straightforward as we would like.

The problem that someone brings may only be the symptom of greater disorder elsewhere. Moreover, the one who is in need, while seeking our advice, may also try their hardest – consciously or unconsciously – to destroy us as we attempt to help them.

Intercession on another's behalf can be a call to engage in a spiritual battle with the forces of darkness. In this instance, the power of evil will also do its best to try and do away with the intercessor. The parish priest is not unfamiliar with the feeling of entering into a situation of pastoral or spiritual counselling on his or her knees (having prayed beforehand) and leaving on hands and knees (having become thoroughly drained of strength and emotion by the demands of others).

There may also be those whom the priest would rather not help, given the choice. But the priest has not been called to die for the healthy but for the sick. In order to get to heaven and to bring it to others we have to die on the cross for our executioners:

> We have to die, as Christ died, for those whose sins are to us more bitter than death – most bitter because they are like our own. We have to die for those whose sins kill us, and who are killed, in spite of our good intentions, by many sins of our own.

(Merton, 1955)

However, this should not prevent us from taking steps to protect ourselves. As we have already noted, a priest suffering from spiritual and emotional exhaustion is no good to anyone and his or her sacrifice when required may be impaired as a result. God makes a considerable investment in the calling of those he would have as spiritual leaders. While the longevity of an individual's ministry is ultimately in the hands of God and often dependent upon the type of ministry undertaken, it is not to be curtailed by overwork. This is a case of 'Into my hands, I commend my spirit'; it is a false form of discipleship which we will be looking at in more detail in the next chapter.

Another danger to avoid is that of taking people on for long-term pastoral counselling. It is not un-Christian to exercise great care before we commit ourselves to counsel others. There will, no doubt, be many who will be helped by our support, while others – for their own reasons – prefer to hold on to their problems and cling to us rather than move forward. On these occasions it is better to pass on the work of intercession to others who can stand by and help, without being as vulnerable to attack. If a minister is sometimes afraid to withdraw support from an individual, this may say more about his or her own needs, a fear of failure or desire to be indispensable. In such a situation the counselling process has become unbalanced, in that the counsellee is being used to meet the personal inadequacies of the counsellor. There is no failure in a priest either asking someone to see them infrequently – it may in fact be the best thing for them in terms of their own personal development – or in the referral of them to another agency that is far better equipped to counsel those with deep-seated problems. If in the prayer of intercession we cannot ourselves remain with someone, there is no reason why, having made the initial contact, we should not allow others to keep watch and pray.

The final area of concern is also to do with the degree of personal involvement. If an intercessor cannot identify with someone – perhaps for reasons of self-preservation – he or she cannot then fulfil the task of intercessory prayer, for, if this prayer is to be effective, then the one who prays should 'feel' something of the pain of the other. This, surely, is one of the reasons why we are called to suffer ourselves. Not so that we can say 'I know how you feel', because this is impossible and patronizing to say the least. But whatever we are with people in pain is greatly enhanced if we, too, have known similar pain, loss or grief and bring these to the art of sympathetic listening. By becoming co-sufferers we are granted a depth of experience and empathy that enable us to relate to others in a helpful and meaningful way.

The priest needs to be careful, however, that in sharing the pain of others he or she is not overcome, and achieving the balance between caring and collapsing under the weight of the burdens of others is not always straightforward.

'To weep with one eye'[1] is a Zen Buddhist-like expression which provides a helpful image to describe the usually appropriate level of involvement in intercession. This is not to say that there may come a time when we are called to give everything to help others. But this is the exception rather than the norm and it is important to tell the difference between the two. In the prayer of intercession, James did indeed make the final sacrifice whereas his brother did not. Both, however, in their respective ministries, embraced the suffering of the world and fulfilled their calling to hold fast in creative tension with the power of redemptive love those for whom Christ died.

NOTES

1 See Psalm 75.8 (the cup of joy) and Isaiah 51.17 (the cup of sorrow) as referred to by William Barclay in his *Commentary on the Gospel of Mark*, St Andrew Press, Edinburgh, 1975, p. 255.
2 cf. M. Scott Peck, *The Road Less Travelled and Beyond*, Random House, London, 1997, p. 194.

REFERENCES

T. Merton, *No Man Is an Island*, Burns and Oates, Tunbridge Wells, 1955 (ninth impression 1993), p. 187.
M. Muggeridge, *Something Beautiful for God*, William Collins, London, 1971, p. 130.
S. Silouan, *Wisdom from Mount Athos*, St Vladimir's Seminary Press, New York, 1975, pp. 21–2.

5

THE PRAYER OF COMPLETE

COMMITMENT

'or be baptised with the baptism that I am baptised with?'
(Mark 10.38)

In this chapter we will be looking at the nature of complete commitment and some practical issues that arise from it. Those who are familiar with the parochial ministry will know how quickly an imbalance between work, home and recreation can, in a relatively short period of time, render the most enthusiastic and imaginative priest exhausted and disillusioned. As the numbers of stipendiary clergy continue to fall, individual priests are asked to cope with an increasingly heavy workload. Despite the growth in lay ministry – which quite rightly has its own integrity and is not simply about helping out the clergy – the parish priest can still feel under siege from the relentless demands of parish life.

What follows, therefore, are some observations and suggestions to help clergy deal with the pressure they frequently live under so that they can retain the excitement and joy of ministry without neglecting their personal lives.

Just as the baptism of Christ was given to James and John, so it is given for the disciple and spiritual leader today for whom there can be no half measures. It is by grace that we have been called rather than through any merit of our own. And by grace we are to perform the duties of discipleship and seek to make the face of Christ known to others that they might see him and live.

This is a vocation to pursue the demands of radical love which places the priest in the midst of the suffering of the world. The priest makes known to the world the demands of God, not by seeking after power or making unrealistic demands but by the pursuit of holiness. This is the path of voluntary suffering, self-denial, humility and obedience.

Such a form of discipleship can be threatened by the needs of the institution and a false desire to put respectability first. Dietrich Bonhoeffer once said that discipleship in the Church in the West seemed to be characterized by 'cheap grace', where the predominant duty of a Christian had become to 'leave the world for an hour or so on a Sunday morning and go to church to be assured that my sins are all forgiven' (Bonhoeffer, 1959). The urgency of the gospel message can be turned into a form of spiritual cosiness designed to dish up a feeling of well-being through undemanding spirituality. In a consumer society, the emphasis is often first on how God can cheer us up rather than on what we can offer him in return for what he has already given. The Church appears to encourage its members at times to lean on God, not so much to discover their true identity in him but to find an emotional support to get them through the week.

The priest is called to help others see the face of Christ not through the rites of religion, which incidentally are meaningless to those on the outside, but through the process of the transfiguration of his or her own life.

This is not a commitment to try and eradicate all human faults by our own efforts, for this endeavour, no matter how worthily pursued, simply leads to greater degrees of spiritual depression due to our innate fallibility. Here we confuse true humility – essentially being 'of the earth' before we can be 'of heaven' – with a self-condemnation which reinforces our state of sin or estrangement from God where we can never be allowed to be our true selves.

Instead, the priest is committed to a contract – or covenant – the basis of which is the unconditional love of God for the world. This is nothing less than becoming completely submerged in the baptism of discipleship that God gives to us. Here we are drawn into a relationship with the Father in which we find ourselves achieving union with the very depths of our selves, the world around us and with him. Holiness is not found in the imposition of the sacraments on people, but in the way they identify and confirm the life of God that is already within. Holiness happens when the Spirit confronts and transforms deep-seated alienation caused by the demons within. In the life of the individual, this may involve, for example, facing up to the consequences of fallen relationships in background and up-bringing which have resulted in a tilt of the axis from self-fulfilment to self-negation. The way in here is not by the superimposition of impossible scriptural ideals but in the discovery of the unconditional love of God in our fallen selves and our fallen selves in God. In order to be with God and at peace with ourselves, we have first to confront the demons that prevent our balanced personal development, such as the fear of rejection that makes us overcompensate by becoming either too loud or too quiet.

The priest has first to help others find and be themselves in God in a process where they are transformed from his image into his likeness, that is from one degree of glory to another (2 Corinthians 3.18). As a consequence, any endeavour to try and be holy should be substituted by the far more important task of concentrating on becoming whole. One of the functions of daily prayer is to stop spiritual leaders from trying to make themselves into the saints they think they should be. We ask instead for help to be ourselves.

The prayer of complete commitment is based not on our complete immersion in church administration, management, fundraising and politics but on the command to love our neighbours as we love ourselves. Yet, we generally find it more straightforward to love God and others rather than embark on the inward journey of self-examination. If, though, we do not first permit God to heal us from within then we will have little authentic love to share with others.

Again we are reminded that it is not selfish but essential that the priest should care for him- or herself. It is not a distortion but the foundation of our ministry. For it is the will of God that we should become whole as the Spirit of creative love operates upon us. The priest has no need to hide behind façades of false personality. Instead, he or she is to die to the inner drives which are aimed at the survival of the fittest and self-preservation at all costs, in order to find the life of the kingdom that comes from the emptying and offering of the self.

The priest or spiritual leader needs to have an understanding of self that is intrinsic to his or her individuality and not dependent upon the needs or applause of others. He or she needs to know how to become real so that this reality might be offered to others. This involves learning how to be the person whom God has created us to become. The priest, therefore, fights against the temptation to become a possession of others in order to prove that he or she is a successful pastor.

If we can preserve the self and allow God to work on and refine it, then we will have something to give to others that will make Christ known to them. This is not the same as working all hours trying to meet impossible demands at the expense of our own lives and of those around us. The priest who is in the process of becoming whole is one who has been given the grace to offer something of God in him- or herself to release the Spirit in others that they, too, might realize and celebrate their potential as children of God.

Being fully committed involves protecting the integrity not only of our own individuality but also that belonging to those whom we love and with whom we live. The reason why so many clergy suffer from exhaustion and family breakdown may well be because they have found it easier to hide from their real selves by becoming immersed in the busyness of trying to be all things to all people except those closest to them.

In this context, four specific areas of commitment worthy of closer scrutiny are: controlling the crowds, the need to be alone, incarnational love, and the cherishing of loved ones.

While direct personal comparisons between the ministry of our Lord and that of the parish priest today are difficult if not impossible, this need not prevent us from making observations concerning similar principles in operation as regards the ministry of the shepherd among the sheep.

Controlling the crowds

Earlier on in the Gospel of St Mark, we read of the longing of the world for healing and the demands this places upon the healer. Relentlessly, the crowd pursues Jesus and his disciples in the evening, and on the following morning, to the door of the house of Simon and Andrew. After healing a leper, Jesus is unable to enter a town openly and while he stayed out in the country 'people came to him from every quarter'. Returning to Capernaum there were so many people that four friends carrying a paralysed man were forced to lower him through the roof to reach Jesus, and as he walked by the Sea of Galilee he was surrounded by people (Mark 1.29—2.17).

James and John will have been caught up in this relentless activity and they would have known that Jesus would regularly seek time alone for himself and to be with those closest to him. It is likely that these two disciples, together with Peter, were singled out to be with Jesus on such occasions more than the others.[1]

Of all the caring professions, the work of the parish priest is the one with the fewest boundaries. Unlike other professions, the people he or she serves are not confined by specific boundaries of time and space. Whenever the priest is at home – whether at work or not – he or she is still perceived as being constantly available.

The priest can feel persecuted by the needs of the crowd at the front door and on the telephone. There are those who think nothing of ringing at eight o'clock in the morning or ten o'clock at night about routine matters. Requests for help vary from those who are seeking the healing power of Jesus to those who want to have their passport photographs signed! This puts enormous and unreasonable pressure on the priest and his or her spouse and family. While people will ring and make an appointment to see their doctor, social worker, dentist and solicitor they will still regularly expect direct contact on their terms from their parish priest. Moreover, the conscientious priest will not wish to put barriers between him- or herself and those in need. The day that he or she is dismissive of the demands of another may well be the time when someone in real need has plucked up the courage to come to the church for the first time, desperate to hear of the love of God.

Despite the crowds who wished to see him in Capernaum, Jesus felt it right to move on to preach the gospel elsewhere. So there is comfort here in that not even the Son of God was tied down by the needs of everyone. Not at this point, at least. There is no condemnation, therefore, in entrusting those whom we cannot at present help to our heavenly Father, for he knows and loves them far more than we ever will.

Additional relief can be found in switching off the front-door bell during times of prayer and rest, together with the judicial use of an answer machine to screen and record calls. It is only right that we should be allowed the opportunity not only to sit down to eat either alone or with our families, but also to sit still for a while afterwards while the food is digested rather than rushing out straightaway to yet another meeting.

There is also the need to establish boundaries wherever possible in the course of a crowded week's work. In one day a parish priest might be involved in taking a school assembly, a funeral, letter-writing and administration, chairing a commit-tee, making decisions with others about policy and planning, and handling unforeseen circumstances of real need that arise without warning. The parish priest has to wear many different hats but if there is no defining line between the different demands, this can lead to frustration and exhaustion. By all accounts, one of the differences between discipleship in first-century Palestine and today is the faster pace of life, together with the variety of the tasks that confront us. There are times when we need to stop and come to terms with what we have just done. We do not always realize how much energy we constantly give to others on a daily basis.

When a priest goes straight from one task to another, his or her emotional and spiritual needs can be forgotten and clerical burnout beckons.

The need to be alone

We should not be afraid sometimes to say 'No' in order to step back to be quiet. Otherwise, we can find that we are constantly trying to meet the expectations of others, at the expense of ourselves. We have to make up our minds what kind of a priest God has called us to be and persevere with this model regardless of the demands of others. It is helpful to discuss our model of priesthood with those we seek to serve so as to give them the opportunity to understand and work with rather than against us. What is certain is that if we do not stand up to the unreasonable expectations of others – often formed from the best intentions in the world – they will eventually do away with us.

It is also important that we feel we are working in the most effective way possible. There is a need to assess regularly whether we are trying to fit too much into any one day or week. Accurate time-keeping is difficult because of the regular stream of unexpected calls on us. Nevertheless, time management is very important in order to give stability to the working day, not only for the priest but also so that he or she can give proper attention to those with whom he or she comes into contact. If a pastoral counselling session is rushed, instead of being its allotted hour, then neither the priest or the counsellee will feel satisfied. If the priest is to appear relaxed for others and attentive to the needs of their situations, this should not merely be the result of skilled acting.

Time purely for personal recreation in the week is also essential. Only if we do justice to our own needs can we enjoy a balanced life and be able to offer an integrated whole to others. This will involve taking time for hobbies and interests without feelings of guilt because we are not working. It will probably also entail taking regular exercise in order to keep fit and relieve stress. A physically fit priest is far more likely to cope with the demands of his or her work.

Time for spiritual retreat and reflection is also of paramount importance. As a result of this, a balanced perspective can be maintained with the opportunity for the Spirit to empower us, replacing the energy that we have given to others. By keeping in regular contact with his or her supervisor, the priest knows that advice and guidance are always at hand from someone who knows the demands of the vocation together with his or her own strengths and weaknesses.

We shall return to our use of time in the last section of this chapter.

Incarnational love

The incarnation reveals at least three ways in which God worked through Christ in order to identify with humanity and help it to rediscover itself and take control of its destiny under him. We can observe these in action as Jesus walked and talked with James and John on the way to Jerusalem.

First, there is the need for Jesus to be true to himself in his relationships with others. Most of those who came across him – including those closest to his heart – seem to have found it almost impossible to understand his real identity and mission until some time after the resurrection. While there were very good reasons for Jesus on occasions not to be open or straightforward in what he did or said, he never pretended to be someone he was not. At times he may have been evasive to prevent others imposing their own judgements on him at the wrong moment in his ministry, but he was nevertheless completely genuine in himself as far as those around him were concerned. He would always say what he meant, rather than what others wanted to hear.

Second, there is the desire to accept others with unconditional love. This does not mean that Jesus necessarily approved of everything his followers said or did. Nevertheless, he accepted them where they were. And from there he gave them the power to reach their full potential as human beings grounded in the Spirit of God. The words of James and John which we are looking at reveal a distortion of the gospel message. And while Jesus shows his exasperation at their inability to understand at times (cf. Mark 8.17ff.), nowhere does this result in his banishing them from his circle. Among his followers were people who had been terrorists, crooked financiers, prostitutes, and wasters. Yet nowhere does he say, 'I will only sit at table with you if you change this and that about yourself first.' Instead he dines with 'publicans and sinners' and from their table challenges them to make decisions that with God they might become whole.

Third, God in Jesus reveals that he both experiences and understands the human condition. He feels our spiritual disorientation, fears, concerns and confusion. This means that the words Jesus spoke came from One who has shared our experience of life including feelings of God-forsakenness. Therefore, when he speaks he does so with a meaning which comes not only from his own heart but also from our heart.

It is because Jesus was full of this love that he was able to respond to the outlandish request of James and John with such tenderness and grace. Moreover, as we have seen and will observe, these aspects of incarnational ministry are also present in the life of the parish priest. They have also surfaced, become accepted and are much in use – though in non-specific Christian terms – in the world of counselling where they are given different names.[2]

The calling of the priest, however, is not so much one to counselling as to a commitment to have the same love as Christ for the fellow-traveller. By this love, we can enable others to look at themselves in such a way that with Christ they can gain control of their lives in the context of their eternal destiny.

What matters here is that the priest or spiritual leader has little hope of producing these three qualities of ministry if the prayer of complete commitment does not release him or her from the cares and concerns of this life. If not, he or she will be prevented from revealing the incarnate Christ to others because of individual preferences and petty likes and dislikes belonging to this world. The perception will not be, then, that the other person has also been made in the image of God. As a result, the priest will react either positively or negatively depending upon whether he or she perceives the other person as a threat or not to his or her security.

From his reply we may understand that Jesus did not primarily address two over-ambitious brothers who threatened to undo much of that for which he stood and was about to die. Instead, he talked on equal terms with them as people in whom the Spirit longed to bring new life. Therefore, in the prayer of complete commitment there is a need to ask for that kind of incarnational love that recognizes Christ in all things and everyone. For prayers to be effective they must operate at the level of the spirit in others as they do for the priest. Then we can be liberated to pray with a freedom we have hitherto not known as we find ourselves unencumbered by vested interests. For if in prayer we only take ourselves seriously, how can God speak through us at the same time as we ignore him in others?

As we have observed, it is difficult to draw the line where the prayers of the priest begin and end. In fact, it has become clear that his or her entire life is a prayer. If, though, there is a difference between prayer and action then our ministry is based on good intentions only and not on God. 'Prayer must be rooted in our life and if our life contradicts our prayers, or if our prayers have nothing to do with our life, they will never be alive or real' (Metropolitan Anthony of Sourozh, 1986). Incarnational love that draws us so closely to one another in mutual acceptance and harmony is not something we achieve by our own efforts. It is a gift from God. And we can only receive it when we surrender ourselves unconditionally to him in daily prayer. Then, and only then, can the Spirit of Christ become incarnate in our lives and ministry.

Cherishing our loved ones

The prayer of complete commitment means cherishing those whom God has given us to share the journey. For some, complete commitment means being totally dedicated to the life, work and witness of the Church to the exclusion of everyone else. Spiritual leaders, however, are called to do justice to all the love with which they have been blessed.

The marriage of a priest and his or her spouse has particular demands made of it. Each couple has to work out its own way of coping with these which may vary from, for example, the partner who is not ordained wanting his or her own life and career, to the partner who is happy to work as an unpaid assistant. On occasions, it may be perceived that the priest is a centre of attention in a community while the spouse might feel that he or she is regarded as insignificant. The result of this can be role confusion at home. And home, of course, is never really this: it does not belong to the couple, is too big to heat properly in the winter and is invaded regularly by well-meaning people who can give the impression that they own the place and frequently forget to wipe their feet – either physically or metaphorically or both – as they enter!

Among many others, there are the problems that arise when both the priest and his or her spouse are treated according to the role they fulfil for others rather than as the people they really are. Their children, too.

If the priesthood is a vocation which is lived out in a life of work, it should in theory be possible for the priest to stop work and be his or her unclerical self at home. It is unlikely that the spouse will want to be treated as a parishioner or a server at the altar of another's calling. In addition, if children are to grow up in a balanced way, they should not have religion forced upon them morning, noon and night. Just as a priest should avoid being dominant at work, so at home he or she should humbly seek to serve the best interests of the other members of the family.

The priest and his or her spouse benefit from a regular assessment of how the balance between work and family, spouse and saint, priest and parent, is being maintained. Inevitably, there will be occasions when at very busy times the family will lose out, but this should be the exception rather than the norm, the situation being redressed as soon as possible. Children grow up quickly, and times of play and sharing should not lightly be cast aside for the sake of others. This is difficult because work and family life are centred on the home. Every time the priest has to go out can be perceived by a young child as a form of abandonment for someone else who is not even a member of the family. On a purely practical basis, it is good for the children if over the course of a week the priest is at home for mealtimes and bedtimes, in addition to playtimes.

Balancing all this is a tall order. Both priest and spouse benefit when a confidante is found with whom they can share the pressure they feel they are under. A general practitioner – sharing similar pressures to do with expectations and public life – who is known to be wise and whose opinions are valued can be indispensable. The next step is not only to listen to, but also to accept advice when it is offered.

It is good to have some shared interests outside work and to set targets for their integration into the week. Even if a family can achieve some very minor goal each day, it will have made a valuable investment in the cause of staying together and of the individuals having had their needs met.

Moreover, when a priest is physically or emotionally drained and of little use to the community, he or she will have even less to offer at home. It should not be forgotten that the family has more right to the affection, love, time and emotional energy of the priest than anyone else, for it is rarely their decision that one member should give so much of him- or herself to others outside the family group. Constant communication and the willingness to listen are of vital importance in the ongoing nurture of our relationship with those upon whom we depend and whose welfare we are dedicated to protect.

On very rare occasions, it may well be that we have to be separated from our families. This might be because a couple was married before one partner became a priest and either one or both change dramatically and decide that the new lifestyle is not one in which they can survive. While no one willingly opts to go through such painful separation and experience of failure, if every effort has been made to keep things together, it is sometimes in the best interests of everyone if an amicable parting of the ways is agreed. While this may be caused by the problems associated with a vocation to spiritual leadership, it is not something which God wishes on us. Should disaster strike, there is the promise of the love and support of the Christian family which – while being no substitute for kith and kin – can help us to find a new home and support as we try to come to terms with our pain (Mark 10.29–30).

Complete commitment to the gospel calls for priest and spouse to keep in touch with each other by praying together. Here, in the peaceful vulnerability of the inner experience of themselves, they can not only learn to speak their minds, but also seek help to deal with their problems. When the issues are church-related, what more appropriate way can there be to channel the issues that concern them other than by praying together? In praying together, a knowledge of God can often produce a sense of the objectivity of a third party, a go-between, for those seeking a different perspective on an area of mutual concern. In God's presence, individuals may well be encouraged to be more open and honest about how they are feeling.

Sometimes, though, there is a need to be sensitive to the fact that when a problem arises, prayer for some can be a symbol of oppression for at least two reasons.

First, it is important that both partners are able to pray in the way that best suits them, rather than either feel they must adopt the approach of the one who may be perceived as the dominant spiritual partner. If, let us say, there are two different approaches or understandings of prayer, then sensitive discussion and negotiation will have to take place to prevent either individual from feeling oppressed and unable to share what is in their hearts either with their partner or with God.

Second, where the cause for concern is to do with the way the priest is living out his or her vocation, the very thought of praying together can exacerbate the situation. If, for example, the balance between home and church life has tipped in favour of the latter and the priest is neglecting his or her family because of endless evening meetings or because they are forever working in the study on their own, then to offer to pray about the problem may be perceived as a resort to yet another church-type activity, when all that the family wants is to spend some time together.

Finally, the spouse of the priest is not only the most faithful supporter but also the most effective critic. For no one on earth knows us better than our spouses. Normally they will notice immediately when we begin to take ourselves too seriously. This can cause us acute pain and embarrassment as we discover we are not as Christ-like as we thought we were! But such comments are not made to bring us down, for in God's scheme of things they are there to refine us and build us up to ever higher degrees of self-awareness and completeness. In this sense a spouse can have the role not only of a partner but also of an angel through whom God speaks, to encourage and cajole the priest as we sometimes skip, at other times trudge, our way to Jerusalem. Here there is a complementarity in love that should be cherished, soaked in prayer and treasured for life.

So much of what has been discussed depends largely upon the need to manage time effectively. This final section deals with the very practical issue of how this might be achieved.

Managing the diary

First of all, it is important to establish that we organize our working days and months, otherwise it is very easy for the diary to rule our lives. Wherever possible we should aim to be proactive rather than always reactive. Much of our work comes in the latter of these two categories particularly in the area of pastoral counselling, and there is little we can do to change this. However, this gives us all the more reason to make sure that we are proactive in the rest of our lives.

It is useful to prioritize the documents of our in-trays and the jobs for the week. If we have unpleasant work to do, then by following it with something pleasant, we give ourselves the opportunity to relax and unwind.

One day each week should be set aside when we do not do any work at all and when we should try and avoid speaking to colleagues or parishioners whenever it is possible and not impolite. If we do not do this, we usually find it is not long before we begin to talk about work. Best of all is to get away from the parish for part or all of the day. If we can go some-where where the chances of being recognized are remote, then we are far more likely to relax.

At the beginning of the month it pays to go through the diary and plan our time day by day. Every eight weeks it is helpful to have a whole day put aside for catching up with overdue paperwork and general administration. While we cannot cover every eventuality, and meetings may well get moved around, a definite structure to the month relieves the stress of having to try and fit everything in on an ad hoc basis. The days we fail to organize are usually those when work takes precedence over family. To avoid this, we can put a line through part of a day for our own recreation which might include time with friends and loved ones.

It is inadvisable to work more than two sessions per day. (A session is a morning, or an afternoon or early evening block of time.) When that is not possible – and it is a very difficult aim to achieve – we should try hard to catch up the lost time in the near future.

Every three months it helps to have a 'weeding' session when we sit down and go through our work and decide what is essential and what is not. Life becomes more manageable when we weed out those things which it is not necessary for us as priests to be doing. A considerable amount of paperwork can be carried out by volunteers, and we all need to delegate.

In addition to the day off each week, we should incorporate two consecutive days off once a month beginning at five o'clock on the preceding evening. It is not possible to unwind adequately in one day and it is not unreasonable to have the equivalent of a weekend off every four or five weeks.

Essential for the maintenance of our spiritual equilibrium is a quiet day every month. On this day, we might spend the time in a retreat centre or some other suitable accommodation, using the time for spiritual purposes only. In addition, a week-long annual retreat that is counted as work and not as holiday is essential.

At the risk of repetition, we should not neglect to rule family and friends into the diary. This sounds rather too formal a way to relate to those close to us, and of course we would not refuse to have anything to do with them outside this time! The act of ruling them in does, however, help to remind us of this priority which otherwise might be taken for granted and forgotten.

At the start of each week, we can undertake the fine-tuning of what we have organized, ensuring again that there is a proper balance between our spiritual life, desk work, visiting, meetings and recreation.

In a busy parish it is legitimate to take six weeks – including six Sundays – a year as holidays and these should be entered into the diary as early as possible.

Feelings of guilt associated with having a justifiable amount of time off need to be balanced by the knowledge that we tend to work very long hours, and the demands on us are considerable. In short, we owe it to God, ourselves and everyone else to stay as fresh as possible. When we are tired it is self-defeating to complain about how hard our life is, saying 'I can't make it any easier because ...'; 'can't' is a word that is often caused by, and surrenders us to, the effects of stress. Even if it means a change to our lifestyle, having identified them we need to work to remove the causes of stress. Merely talking about them does not make them go away. Doing something does. Stress often comes as a result of feelings of helplessness which surface when we feel that someone else is in control of us and our time.

NOTES

1 See Mark 1.16–19; 3.16; 9.2–8; 14.33; and Luke 8.51.
2 Namely 'congruence', 'unconditional positive regard' and 'empathetic understanding'. Cf. Carl Rogers, *On Becoming a Person*, Constable and Co., 1967, pp. 282–4.

REFERENCES

D. Bonhoeffer, *The Cost of Discipleship*, SCM Press, London, 1959, pp. 35–47.

Metropolitan Anthony of Sourozh, *The Essence of Prayer*, Darton, Longman and Todd, London, 1986, p. 121.

6

THE PRAYER OF 'YES'

'We are able.'

(Mark 10.39)

At whatever moment we give ourselves to the service of God, be it at a specific time earlier on in our lives and ministry or at the start of each new day, we take a step into the unknown. The prayer of 'yes' to the discipleship of Christ involves both enthusiastic acceptance and faithful determination. James and John voiced a desire to give their lives completely to the way of God in the world. They were not diverted from their aim by any reproof of Jesus, or the gradual dawning realization that in fact they knew very little indeed about what lay ahead.

To give in to a deep sense of vocation to the priesthood can be both an exciting and frightening experience. While it is, above all, an assent to the love of God, it bestows deep peace and great uncertainty.

Typically, the story involves a strong conviction – felt at the deepest level – that 'this is what God wants me to do'. There is an inner compulsion which the individual senses will not let him or her go. It is usual to test such a call by trying to ignore it, perhaps in the hope that it might go away. After a period of time it becomes clear that the vocation is permanent, and, while other vocations and lifestyles might have been preferred as being more attractive or less demanding, peace of mind and spirit will not remain if the voice within is denied.

Why God should choose the men and women he does is

usually a mystery, not least to the congregations they seek to serve! An ordinary life is made extraordinary – sometimes out of all character to what has gone before – because of a 'feeling' that no one can prove and a God who is apprehended by faith. A priest is not someone who has led a blameless life, or ever will. He or she may not have been a regular worshipping member of the Church, nor even have been regarded as particularly grounded in the spiritual side of life. Yet there are raw qualities within the person that are needed by God in a particular way for this work.

It is not the priest, however, nor a vocations board, nor anyone else for that matter, who first informs a person that they have a vocation. Instead, it is usual for the individual – independent of anyone else – to give in to a call that has been sensed for some time. The vocation is then assessed objectively by others, but any would-be priest who answers the question 'Why ordination?' with a response that indicates it was his or her idea in the first place, has perhaps yet to understand the true origin of his or her calling.

In the case of James and John, they – like us – had been 'chosen' even before they had been born (Ephesians 1.3–5). The spiritual ancestry of the human race has its origins within the timeless love of God and ultimately, therefore, before the creation of the world. And if men and women are called to this type of service by grace, there is no reason why God's decision should not have been made well before we could ever conceive of it. The priesthood, then, is not comprised of those who themselves think that this way of life might match their abilities and interests, but of those who have responded to a specific movement of the creative Spirit of the universe.

To sense such a vocation – and to have it verified – provides a very special moment which few, even after many years, cannot recall without great clarity.

The original assent is often followed by a faithful arrogance – not unlike that of James and John – that purely by our own efforts we are going to change the world for Christ, thereby turning the nature of Christian ministry on its head. Once the real burden of the cross is felt, however, faithful determination takes over and the priest begins to emerge.

The prayer of 'yes' has far-reaching implications, usually unimagined at the time of ordination. It is an agreement to something which is both temporal and supra-temporal. It is not an assent to go off and work on our own, but to have our lives aligned in harmony with the Spirit. In this way, we begin to co-operate with God in the salvation of the world from the death of self-obsession. We become inextricably bound up with the history of the salvation of the world from its creation to its final redemption.

This brings a new perspective to parish life which rather than being an end in itself is viewed as part of one spiritual continuum from earliest times. For the gospel is not primarily to do with the maintenance of the fabric of an institution but with the promotion of eternal life. This in itself is not a message about longevity to be sold to a society that seeks to invent its own divinity but the offer to live within the life and love of God in this world and the next.

Eternal life has at least two consequences for the priest in that he or she has to learn the value of irrelevance and, paradoxically, how to make the past, present.

The value of irrelevance

The highly laudable aim of trying to make relevant a 2000-year-old faith – that lays great emphasis on such things as the symbolic meaning behind seed-planting and sacrifice – to a world of silicon chip and cyberspace hides a blasphemy. For relevance in the realm of the spiritual comes only as a gift from God. No amount of up-to-date management practice or market research and analysis – while important for running the institution – will add one jot to the meaning and efficacy of covenantal love. Relevance in mission comes only when it is shot through with the incarnate love of Christ. When this is not the case then others will rush to see only the empty tomb of our worldly dreams. So from time to time we might ask ourselves, 'Who is it that you are looking for?' For only when we come to acknowledge the death of our noble ambitions, and turn to face the risen Christ standing where we least expect to find him, will others come to know that incarnate love for themselves. Eternal life calls us to do away with every fabrication and pretence and to understand and accept ourselves within a love that is itself without temporal or spacial limit.

While we are presumptuous in thinking that we can make the gospel relevant, we have not been called to do nothing. If relevance rests with God, the task of the priest is to help others relate to the gospel and to Christ himself. This is best achieved not by a didactic, authoritarian approach but by a quiet and constant questioning of how others feel and believe. The priest facilitates the developing relationship between Christ and believer, not in constantly giving answers but by offering advice when invited so that, retaining their personal integrity, others may own their own faith. Stepping back as the bond of love increases, the priest allows the spiritual life and gifts of the other person to be identified and utilized. Sooner or later the priest – who may have played an important part at the start of the process – will take a back seat as the skills of the convert develop, becoming increasingly irrelevant in many ways as the other takes responsibility for his or her own discipleship.

This process can only happen by the grace of God and not by any kind of vicarious sanctification by the good works of the priest. Having facilitated it for one, the priest then moves on to another who has been sent to repeat the process. This is not to say that the ministry of an individual will not be cherished by grateful parishioners but that our own contribution will be balanced by the authentic life of Christ we have helped to nurture in others. This is a timeless endeavour founded on the operation of the Spirit whose primary aim is not to produce another contributor to the parish finances but someone who has claimed their identity as a son or daughter of God. However, if this is the result of our outreach then it is very likely that not only the spiritual but also the fiscal accounts of the church will benefit!

Here the prayer of 'yes' is concerned less with delivering religion and more with bringing reality to our way of life. Here it is that we learn to relate to the Creator God who gave himself as Spirit and Son in the processes of creation and recreation. The Church is not somewhere to go to run away from the world in an attempt to arrest the hands of the evolutionary clock. For the priest is called to enable others to engage with life at its deepest level in the timeless possibilities of ongoing creation. By so doing, he or she will help to maintain a prophetic voice in a rapidly changing world about what will lead to eternal life and what will lead to everlasting damnation.

Having consciously become a part of the spiritual continuum of the emergence of covenant love in the world, the priest – in common with other Christians – has an indissoluble link with those who have laboured for the same purpose in previous generations. The presence of a parish church is due as much to the faith of the early Fathers as it is to more recent generations. The work and witness of each individual priest is of enormous significance for the progress of the kingdom but it is also a mere 'blip' on the screen of spiritual progress. This is not to devalue the vocation of the priest at all for, without this particularly priestly life ordained by God, the progress of the covenant will be retarded. To refer to it as transitory and almost unnoticeable is to place its unique value within the eternal purposes of God. We play our part as best we can for as long as we are given, but our eternal fulfilment is not in a successful summer fayre but in the fellowship of the saints. It is perhaps particularly helpful to remember this following an unsuccessful summer fayre!

Making the past present

The current of love which is the creative drive behind the evolution of the human spirit is the same yesterday, today and forever (Hebrews 13.8) and the world's ability to perceive and receive God changes and develops as each successive generation discovers more about the reality behind all things. As we have seen – contrary to the practices of commercial progress and development – when Christians make the past present in faith we find that constant in the love of God which lends the covenantal perspective for living with the here and now.

In the Eucharist the priest enables the people to take part in the *anamnesis* of Christ, remembering in such a way as to make the past present today. By physical and spiritual means the words of the Last Supper are presented in such a way as to open heaven to earth, uniting us with the saints of the Church past in prayerful adoration of God and in the furtherance of his kingdom.

This is a strange tension with which to live. On the one hand there is a desire and need to be a child of one's own generation while mediating the unique revelation of another. Dog collars, cassocks and stoles do not symbolize a turning away from the present in an attempt to recreate the past. Instead, they represent the way we treasure that inheritance of faith which can unlock the meaning of the present. On occasions there may surface a desire to turn the clock back to some imagined 'safer' time when theology and spirituality seemed less complicated and demanding. But this is to ignore the necessary ongoing growth to maturity of the Christian life that is essential for the fulfilment of the kingdom. While it would be possible to turn back the theological clock, this could only be done in the knowledge that it would never again tell the right time.

Imbalance in personal and spiritual development occurs when we cherish the past to the detriment of the reality of today. For we have not been called to live in either the past or the future. In common with all those who have gone before us, we can only live, minister and relate to others in the present moment. It is this living with God and others in the novelty of the present, as co-creators of redemptive love in covenantal relationship with the source of all authentic love, which makes Christian life and ministry so exciting. The past does not become real today by the mere act of vivid remembrance but by the interaction of the creative love of Christ on our spirits in our own time. Reality is found when the truth of the present is not only discovered in Christ but also explored in all its implications for the way we live today. While we can learn from the past, it is always in the present moment that we are in relation to others. In the face of the often abrasive demands the Spirit makes of us, we seek to discover the implications of covenantal love here and now as we help to form the future in creative dynamic with God.

To make Christ available to others in Holy Communion, therefore, is not to make the past real in itself but to make today real by perceiving and receiving eternity and the creative Word of the universe in the present.

Here especially the prayer of 'yes' allows the priest to sit light to conformity to current social and religious trends and pressures. Here we stand in the eternity of the love and self-offering of God which can be as real now as it was for James and John as they walked with Christ.

Keeping the sacred in time

Knowledge of this produces a dogged determination to play our part – as best we can and for as long as we can – in that kind of life nothing can destroy which Mechtild of Magdeburg once described as 'all things being in God and God in all'.

Finding expression for the timeless nature of this vocation brings the newly ordained priest heavily down to earth! While we are using the conversation of James and John with Christ on the way to Jerusalem as an analogy, practical considerations will soon dissipate any early morning mist of romanticism that might persist. As with the first disciples, we have to marry together what is eternal with what is transitory. While the newly ordained priest may find that the earth has been caught up in the fire of the eternity of limitless love, he or she soon discovers the need to manage earth time effectively in a busy parish life.

A well-known secular priest of the Russian Orthodox Church, St John of Kronstadt (1994), who with his wife Elizabeth exercised a prayerful ministry of great magnitude, principally during the nineteenth century, counselled his fellow-priests as follows: 'We must preach that Christ came down to earth in order to lift us up to heaven . . . and that we must value time, filling it with as many good works as possible, in order to win eternity.'

To fill time with holy endeavour is not to become over-busy in the practical support of others, for there is no quicker way of quenching the life of the Spirit. It is important to understand the sacred possibilities in every moment.

To value time in this sense is to develop the necessary balance between what the New Testament calls *chronos* – the time of the watch that ticks its way in weeks, months and years – and *kairos* where the seasons of the Spirit can suddenly break into our lives. While no longer confined by *chronos*, the priest has to live with it. How it is handled will largely determine the way in which God can bring about the emergence of the life of the Spirit according to his will.

Chronos and *kairos*, however, are not two distinct areas of life which do not relate to one another. Effective management of the demands of work leads to a more settled existence with time for personal reflection and the opportunity to hear the 'still small voice'. But times of divine disclosure can also take place when we are extremely busy.

Perhaps this is what was behind St John of Kronstadt's advice concerning the need to 'value time'. As soon as we take time management seriously, we inevitably move from a predominantly economic to a more spiritual appreciation of the day. Life is a precious gift from the Giver of Life and nobody knows how long it will last. So, having imposed some order onto life, we need to treasure the sacred possibilities inherent in every moment of the history and development of the cosmos and, indeed, the universe.

Since the earliest days of the Christian tradition to which St John of Kronstadt belonged, the appreciation of the presence of God at all levels of created reality has been of fundamental importance. The Orthodox Church has always been deeply concerned with the way humanity regards and treats the environment. Salvation is not just about the future of humanity but also about the healing of the natural world, seen vividly in the story of the transfiguration of Jesus.

The story of the bush that caught fire before Moses reminds us now that wherever we walk in terms of God's vocation for our lives – lay or ordained, committed Christian or not – the present is always pregnant with the Divine presence that has since been revealed specifically in the incarnate Word. So the vocation of the parish priest is not just to faithful congregations but to the whole life of the parish, for the cosmos that is on fire with the Spirit of God is itself the ongoing history of creation and salvation.

To say 'yes' to God in this way is to have one's eyes opened and sight restored so that we see not only the physical but also perceive the spiritual within and beyond (cf. Mark 4.11–12). Having committed ourselves to the Divine purpose, we can contemplate – gaze on – reality and be led to the inner Word which constantly calls all life into being. Every moment then becomes sacred, not in the sense that it should be ecclesiastically compartmentalized, separated and venerated, but in the celebration that it contains the eternity of the life and love of God. To value time in this way is to know that the kingdom of heaven

87

and the reality of this world are not as far away from each other as we might have otherwise imagined. It is to know, also, that we are surrounded by the communion of saints in the holy endeavour of salvation and that everything we say, do, think and feel is of eternal consequence. To 'win eternity' is not, therefore, a reward in another life for being a good disciple in the here and now. Rather, it has to do with clawing back authentic life and love from the darkness whose constant aim is to deny the world such honesty and purity of being. Yet this 'yes' is not only to see and perceive, but also to understand.

Sight and understanding

Understanding comes only to those who can assent to the Divine purpose of life. To hold out on vocation is to deny ourselves the chance to see how life makes most sense when we co-operate with God. To put off the prayer of 'yes' because of a lack of knowledge is to withhold oneself from the revelation that renews the mind by the development of an ever-deepening spiritual awareness. Knowledge that is defined purely by the parameters of like-minded people without recourse to a higher Being defines *kairos* only in terms of a secular definition of *chronos*. Understanding comes when we realize – not as a result of the accumulation of facts but from a disposition of the spirit – that ultimate meaning can only be found within *kairos*.

Understanding inevitably leads to participation in the life of God where the sacred nature of the moment is revealed as the meeting place of God and humanity, order and confusion, identity and anonymity, heaven and earth.

In the Gospels, one of the most vivid pictures we have of one – like ourselves – who came to value time in this way is that of the woman who, having suffered haemorrhages for twelve years, came to Jesus (Mark 5.25–34).

According to popular belief at the time, the woman would have thought that her blood contained not only her physical but also her spiritual life. In her constant bleeding, therefore, she was a person whose life was always running away from her. (Moreover, she lived in a culture that often interpreted a person's state of health in terms of it being a result of God's judgement for good or bad behaviour.) Despite the best efforts of humanity, she could not hold on to life.

Consequently, she approached Jesus not because of an understanding that comes from knowledge but from a perception of faith that follows on from the prayer of 'yes'. Having accepted his Truth, she knew that in a moment she would be well. In a moment she would meet with one who not only could give but also could sustain life. By contrast, the majority of the crowd that thronged around Jesus was inquisitive, even interested, without yet being committed. So at this moment, it was only to this woman – a religious and social outcast because of her considered personal impurity – that healing was given. At the time, the majority of the crowd seemed focused on the physical journey to the house of Jairus and a discussion of the facts, ignoring the inner spiritual path. Theirs was the prayer of 'yes, but not yet' by which many vocations are lost.

In meeting with Jesus – among the crowded ambitions, interests and demands of daily living – the woman was given the power to hold on to life. As a result of her assent to the Divine purpose for herself, she would never again be able to be with others without remembering the possibilities for life that always existed among them. She would have realized that what was true for herself was true for everyone else. If only they had the time.

As the parish priest lives out the consequences of the continuous prayer of 'yes', there is the potential at any time – and all of the time – for him or her to be at this meeting place with others and with God. If we push past the crowd of pressures that seek to obscure Christ's love from the world, we can find his potential for life in a handshake, in the celebration and dedication of new life at baptism, in the laughter of children in a school playground, in the sacred nature of the covenant of love in marriage, in the person who has lost God's purpose for them in the myriad demands of daily living, in the one who is successful yet sits in the pews while still searching for the truth, in the lonely and dispossessed, in the arrogant and aggressive, and in the tears of grief.

The prayer of 'yes' is both giving in to God's vocation and an affirmation of his life in and for the world. The 'daily round and common task' are set afire because of the Divine possibilities this brings in every encounter as we are called to be with others to reach out and touch, meet and hold on to the life that God alone gives and sustains.

Having said all this there is a sense, however, in which there is no such thing as a present moment in the service of God. As soon as it comes, it inevitably passes into an experience of conscious awareness which itself is a synthesis of past, present and the possibilities of the future. To be committed to the sacred moment is to treat the present with great respect as the context of the history of God's vocation while being continuously propelled – or rather impelled by the Spirit within – to new possibilities of creativity.

Therefore, as part of the task of co-operating in the prayer of 'yes', the priest is called constantly to use his or her gifts and abilities to the full. Yet as we are caught up and carried along in the history of the love of God, we can undervalue the gifts that have been given to us. Faithful obedience does not mean we wait for God to do everything! Having said 'yes', though, contemplation of the apparent enormity of the task that confronts us can lead to a significant lack of self-confidence.

Saying 'yes' to our gifts

In the face of this challenge, an over-reliance on the laudable desire to be led by the Spirit in our service of God can lead to a false form of spiritual dependence. The process of dying to self is not so much a way we cease to exist, but one in which new spiritual heights and depths are discovered concerning the way we participate in the Divine life.

To leave absolutely everything with God may sound like living by complete faith. Yet this can become a way by which we refuse to face up to situations that are causing life to run away from ourselves and those to whom we minister. Leaving everything to God in prayer should not be an escape from the harsh realities of life. We do not want to act so we seek a plausible reason why we should not. We like to pray that God will intervene in our lives in some miraculous way, thus leaving the responsibility for change entirely with him without any cost to ourselves. In the meantime, the situation about which we are praying steadily deteriorates. Such is the thinking of the spoilt child.

While Divine intervention does occur in dramatic ways from time to time, it is rare. More often we are shown a way out, or a way through, that we have to take. Here the opportunity is given for increased emotional and spiritual growth and a greater depth of love. When we have recognized this, we are more likely to be open to guidance concerning the part we are to play in bringing about change:

> God's will for us is not only that we should be the persons He means us to be, but that we should share in His work of creation and help Him to make us in to the persons He means us to be. Always, and in all things, God's will for me is that I should shape my own destiny, work out my own salvation, forge my own eternal happiness, in the way He has planned for me.
>
> (Merton, 1955)

If we ignore the gifts we have been given that can be used for the building up of the Body of Christ, we deny the God-given potential of our human nature. It is a false definition to describe natural gifts as second to gifts in ministry when in fact it is God who blesses his people both with spiritual insight and with humour, music, leadership ability and so on. From the place where we meet with Christ, he brings us to that point of full personhood whereby we learn to love and have confidence in ourselves. From here we can with a clear conscience celebrate our personal gifts which themselves come from the Spirit. To these may be added other specific spiritual gifts which equip us to fulfil certain roles and functions in the building up of the Body of Christ.

The Jesus Prayer, 'Lord Jesus Christ, Son of God, have mercy on me a sinner', which has from the earliest times been at the centre of the spiritual life of the Orthodox Church, achieves a natural balance between dedication and celebration. By the constant repetition of the words the believer is bound to God by an unceasing movement of prayer. To take the words at face value might convince some of their near total lack of worth so that they dare not approach God at all. Yet Orthodox Christians stand rather than kneel for the Liturgy because they believe that God by his grace in Jesus Christ has granted dignity to humanity to approach him without fear. Here is a clear expression of the relationship between ongoing penitence for sin and the need for forgiveness together with the celebration of new life and faith. The maintenance of this prayerful balance produces spiritual equilibrium in the life and work of the priest and in the offering of his or her gifts.

Self-consciousness can now be replaced by confidence. Any perceived need to fit some imagined, ecclesiastical mould of false holiness is discarded in favour of a high degree of self-respect in the service of God. This is not to suggest that God calls the priest to give him- or herself to the world by a form of spiritual élitism or by any way that sets the priest apart or – God forbid – above others, but by that way of human becoming that comes from knowing Christ.

Priests, therefore, become imitators of Christ, not because they are good at acting, but because lives lived in his presence reflect his love in the world. Like Jacob and his successors in the faith, James and John, we learn how to walk not on our own but with God in such a way that neither is diminished by lack of respect and both find mutual fulfilment in a celebration and salvation of life.

In common with James and John, the prayer of 'yes' will invariably mean that the priest will be required to enter new and sometimes hostile environments. In such situations, he or she might wonder what gifts they possess that are relevant to the situation that faces them.

Yet whatever the priest requires to meet a new challenge into which he or she has been led by God, is invariably given at the right time. When looking at the road ahead, the need to plan life according to the gifts and abilities we feel we possess is thereby removed. By contrast, the challenge implicit in the 'yes' is to be like leaves blown in the divine wind (*ruach*), prepared to be taken wherever the Spirit leads and content in the knowledge that in this way we will fulfil all that is required of us. As we walk in time with Christ, we can therefore with justified confidence make the words of James and John our own as we respond to our vocation and say, 'We are able!'

REFERENCES

T. Merton, *No Man Is an Island*, Burns and Oates, Tunbridge Wells, 1955 (ninth impression 1993), p. 56.

St John of Kronstadt, *Counsels on the Christian Priesthood: Selected Passages from My Life in Christ*, ed. W. Jardine Grisbrooke, St Vladimir's Seminary Press, New York, 1994, p. 83.

7

THE PRAYER OF THE WORLD

'But to sit at my right hand or at my left hand is not mine to grant, but it is for those for whom it has been prepared.'
(Mark 10.40)

The principal aim thus far has been to look at the work of the priest or spiritual leader in the context of the worshipping community he or she seeks to serve. In this last chapter we will look briefly at his or her call to the world beyond the boundaries of the baptized community.

The final words of Jesus in the conversation with James and John on the road to Jerusalem serve to remind us that there is no room in the kingdom of God for élitism on behalf of those who suppose their ordained life and ministry might in some way be of a superior quality to that of the lay person.

Mother Mary Clare (1981) once affirmed that the Christian life is a 'unity in baptism'. There is 'no double standard of higher or lower vocations, there is no praying minority in an otherwise activist Church, no religious priesthood and professional religious with a secularised laity ... There is only the unity of prayer, the gift of God available for all as he wills.'

Yet we can go further than this. For it is the calling of the Church in general, and the parish priest in particular, to listen to and participate in the prayer not just of the Church but of the world as well.

Given the wider vocabulary that theologians employ today, the Church can perhaps speak with greater eloquence of the ongoing life of the Spirit at every level of reality. We can now appreciate that the physical evolution of the planet – indeed of the universe – is also and at the same time the history of the emergence of the Spirit through creation. We understand afresh what it means to say that God and humanity are held together in a contract – or covenant – of creative love by which the whole of creation is called to reach fulfilment.

In Christ we see the God who sustains not only those who think themselves to be religious but also the cosmos as a whole. In the episode of the woman caught in adultery, Christ affirms the worth – and hence the spiritual identity – of the woman living outside the law. In almost utter silence, the Word sweeps aside the arguments of those who apparently were more concerned with the preservation of religion than with the salvation of the world (John 8.1–11).

Moreover, the Church that was founded in the name of Christ, while sometimes referred to as the 'ark of salvation', is not an institution to be regarded as separate from the rest of the world. It is, rather, a community of those who have been called out of the world – away from the priorities of itself – in order to 're-enter' the world and be about the priorities of God. The Church cannot exist without the world any more than the world can exist without it. To separate the two is to perpetuate a false dualism that has be-devilled the work of faithful Christians for centuries. The Church has been called to wash the feet of the world and in turn to be evangelized by it.[1]

Yet spiritual leadership frequently appears to be more con-cerned with drawing people into Sunday worship and the preservation of the institution. It does not often appear to proclaim that everybody is made in the image of God and that the voice of the Spirit can be heard outside as well – if not at times better – as inside the Church. The bedrock of the ministry of Christ can be seen in his time in Galilee where he spoke in terms of the fulfilment of the Divine potential for everyone and everything. Here is God's answer to the prayer of the world for identity, meaning, security and hope. Only then did Christ travel to Jerusalem to take on those spiritual leaders who had confined the message of covenant love to the criteria of economic and political survival.

The Church is the custodian of the revelation of God to humanity that reached its climax in the life, teaching, death and resurrection of Jesus Christ. In the living out of its vocation to make this known through its communities of faith, however, it would be erroneous – to say the least – for the Church to presume that it holds the monopoly on God's activity in the world. A balanced ministry means that the parish priest works with the Christian laity not only to look after the local church but also to bring about spiritual integration with the life of the community they seek to serve.

So the prayer of the Church is not the only prayer that is uttered. There are the prayers of other religions together with the prayers of those with no specific religion at all. The spirituality of others is not invalid simply because it is outside the body of those who have been baptized. We forget at our peril that it is only by creative dialogue between everyone who is engaged in an honest search for the truth that the world can look to the future with any realistic hope of peace.

This is not to deny, though, as has always been the case, that there will inevitably be false spiritualities that have to be opposed. The balanced spiritual development of humanity is by no means assured, and lines between that which is authentic and inauthentic have to be drawn for the good of all.

The parish priest, as one who presents the revelation of God in Christ, holy Scripture and Tradition, may therefore understand the world to be the Church. This liberates him or her from focusing only on one branch of the Christian family which, by spending too much time on looking after its own interests, can quickly become separated from the community it seeks to serve.

How, then, may the priest perceive the existence of the prayer of the world and in what ways – within his or her own specific calling – can he or she participate in it?

Perceiving the prayer of the world

Preferring the Irenaean picture of a world that is in the process of becoming we tend to find unworkable today the Augustinian picture of a static cosmos where much is pre-ordained and free will has been lost. In opting for the former, we recover sight of the sacramental nature of all life and its potential to develop towards divinity. As a result, we can see that while God gives himself in Christ in a special and unique form in the Eucharist, he is also present and active wherever the food of life is shared.

In order to perceive the prayer of the world there has to be an awareness of the dynamic energy of God in creation. This has been a constant theme in the Christian faith and was clearly expressed in the writing of Maximus the Confessor (580–655) in the Orthodox East.

Maximus held that the mystery of God's embodiment in the world could be countenanced through the recognition of the existence of his uncreated energies or *logoi*. These are transcendent in origin but immanent in function as the divine principle of life in every aspect of created reality. The *logoi* provide the purpose for different species in the overall plan of God which is the unification – without the elimination of diversity – of all things in him. Their progress towards their goal – the salvation of the world – is hindered by sin and fractured relationships. The *Logos* is himself the many *logoi* and they are him although he is not diminished in any way by their variety. Humanity is called to participate in their life or energies without being assumed into the Divine nature thereby avoiding any claim to equality with God.[2]

In the West there has been a tendency to describe these energies of God in action in terms of his life, power or purpose. Instead of using Logos terminology we might prefer to describe God's creative energy in the world in terms of the operation of the Divine Spirit. Jesus – the visible likeness of the invisible God – was full of this Holy Spirit without hindrance or restriction in his fulfilled humanity and complete divinity.

To conceive of God in terms of his creative energy in the cosmos made flesh in the One we call the Word of God, however, is to provide a vivid picture whereby we may understand the Pauline affirmation that in the renewal of human nature national, cultural and religious differences cease to be of importance as 'Christ is all and in all' (Colossians 3.11). Moreover, modern science describes physical reality as networks of energy where the molecular composition of people and objects consists of the same building blocks. According to how they are arranged, they can produce rocks, trees, animals or human beings.

As the energy of the Word of God both causes and sustains creation, it is in him that we 'live and move and have our being' (Acts 17.28) in the total experience of life. These words – spoken in Athens by Paul to those regarded as pagans – affirm the cosmic Christ as the ground of being. (Paul precedes this remark by pointing out that God does not live in 'shrines made by human hands', a misunderstanding it is easy for the Church to slip into as soon as it starts, at least subconsciously, to equate God with a building in an exclusive manner.) Moreover, Paul completes this picture of cosmic spirituality when he refers to creation as groaning with labour pains as it, too, seeks the freedom that comes from the fulfilment of the Divine potential that lies within (Romans 8.22).

To perceive the prayer of the world, then, is to look constantly beneath the surface of physical reality. To reach this level of prayer is to have the ability to contemplate the cosmic Christ everywhere and in everything in the task of redeeming pain, as the world seeks authentic self-expression without hindrance, and union with God. The Christ of the Church meets with, complements, gathers up and then gives meaning to the Christ of the world (Ephesians 1.22–23). The words and ways of humanity then become either signs of this redemptive activity or its obituary.

This recognition of the Spirit in all things disarms us of that power we like to exercise through subject–object relationships. We have a tendency to separate the Church from the world, the baptized from the unbaptized, the saved from the damned, in a hierarchical manner. From this position we can be quick to patronize those who we feel are beneath our position. The abuse of power in this way has often been at the heart of the world's suspicion of the Church.

By contrast, the priest or spiritual leader is called to be the servant of the Spirit in the world. As God in Christ relates to the world by surrendering himself in its service, so the priest is called to help love to triumph through the sacrifice of inauthentic power.

We are called, however, not only to contemplate such a Christ-like life, but also to make it incarnate in our own lives by working with and living by the same transforming power of resurrection love that brought new life from the death of Christ (Ephesians 1.15–23). If we can see the Spirit as God's creative energy in the cosmos, then the task of the priest is to lead others to recognize and make real their vocation in the developing history of the fulfilment of the possibilities and purposes of creative love.

Distinctions between sacred and secular have nothing to do with definitions drawn by the boundaries of ecclesiastical authority. Instead, contemplative prayer 'sees' the presence of Divine energy within all levels of created reality, leaving us with the unavoidable conclusion that all life is sacred. In this context, the term 'secular' applies to those who fail to see this prayer of God in the world. For the Christian, creative love is the only power that counts. Faithful obedience is rendered powerless when it ignores, looks down on or even despises the Spirit in the world. While closer than most to Jesus, even James and John at this stage appear to have been secular in their understanding of mission.

Leaving religious definitions aside, the priest calls others to see that wherever the Divine energies of creation are frustrated in their task of causing love to flourish, there is a need to act. The demons that threaten to distort and destroy life are not confined to the self-imposed realm of religious people. Christ uses the same word to calm a storm as he does to bring peace to a troubled human life.[3]

By working to remove all that impedes the resurrection of the world and its progress towards its final ascension into the source of all authentic love and life, we engage in mission in its widest sense.

The priest, with others, wages spiritual warfare on all those who wield power without love, engaging with the world so that in the myriad 'choices' made every moment in the evolution of the planet, life is encouraged to turn out right rather than turn out wrong. Where the latter occurs, he or she is there to offer support from a perspective born from the insight that from death comes life.

The parish priest identifies with the prayer of the world, in the desire of every species to flourish and in the hopes of humanity as it bears the prayer of God through joy and pain, success and frustration, dreams and disillusionment. This includes the living energy of those who perhaps will hardly ever darken the door of a church but who nevertheless have a valid spirituality that has its origins in God. These people may never be able to say the Nicene Creed, yet nevertheless have much to teach those who would speak about what God in Christ wants for the world. Unaccustomed to sitting in pews, they will be found in everyday places such as pubs, offices and clubs. Most of the time they are ignored. Regarded as being 'not of our flock' they are often closer to God than many who meet the criteria of organized Christianity.

To sit at the right- or left-hand side of God, therefore, is for all those for whom it has been prepared, namely those who respond positively to the potential of Christ wherever, by grace, they have been granted the opportunity.

Having identified the prayer of the world, we now move to identify specific ways in which the priest may participate with it in the lives of others.

Participating in the prayer of the world

The task of the Christian minister is to tread with care in the process by which he or she co-operates with God to make real and visible the incarnate Christ who already lives within others. If the recognition of the Spirit in others is replaced by religious inquisition, there is a real danger that when Christ is crucified in the prayer of the world his people may never witness his resurrection. The ability to help others progress from a knowledge of Christ in the womb to the enjoyment of his incarnate life, comes from deep and often difficult prayer on their behalf. We see this in Paul's prayer to the church in Galatia: 'My little children, for whom I am again in the pain of childbirth until Christ is formed in you' (Galatians 4.19).

Immersed in the depths of a contemplative life that locates Christ in the fabric of reality, the priest then carries the prayer of the world with him- or herself to unite it with the prayer of the Church. This involves something more than the creative tension of intercessory prayer. For it is here, in the individual life of the priest, that the histories of the world and Church are brought to bear on one another in the pursuit and passion of salvation. This is a weight that threatens to crush for it frequently bears the frustration and lack of fulfilment of all stillborn life. Here patience above all else is required, together with an understanding of the grace that is available to get us through. Here also is the joy of being alongside others in their loving, recreating, yearning, weeping, dying and rising.

While it is an enormous privilege for a priest to be allowed to participate in the prayer of the world, the approach by which this can be achieved is all important. Contemporary society sees as contradictory a declared intention to reach out in healing love which is at the same time coupled with a perceived desire to convict, pronounce guilty and condemn others. While people are prepared to agree that they share in the spiritual contamination of a world that has fallen out of love with its Creator, few are prepared to accept that they should bear the guilt of the mistakes of previous generations. Current perceptions of corporate responsibility do not usually reach this far.[4]

It is of fundamental importance, then, to listen attentively to the voice of Christ in the world. Prayerful listening to the stories of others without the imposition of the paraphernalia of inherited religion enables a dialogue between equals to take place. Either party involved should feel safe and unthreatened by the background, views, faith or personal agenda of the other. Mutual acceptance and the development of faith can then take place. This approach should be reflected in worship where the sacraments of the Church, instead of imposing grand ideas about God, gather up the life of the Spirit inherent in the life of the world. If the sacraments are allowed to acquire an almost 'magical' quality, required by the believer to escape the implications of a guilt most people have already discarded, then little real contact is made which will enhance life where it is lived by the majority of people today.

It follows, then, that those who do not normally attend, yet who come to be married or bring their children for baptism, should be welcomed with generous thanksgiving for having brought God into the church with them. For while, clearly, he is there in the worshipping community, he is not present in any exclusive manner. As we have seen above, it is not the job of the priest to impose Christ onto others but to recognize, welcome and enable his life to develop in them. To make assumptions that God is not already present in a deeply loving relationship where the partners involved have decided to covenant their lives to each other, is to deny the truth behind the New Testament verse often quoted in marriage services that 'God is love and those who abide in love abide in God and God abides in them' (1 John 4.16). If God is the source of all authentic love, it follows that he has been at work in such a couple's life long before a request is made for a marriage in church where in public they will give thanks to God for the gift of their love and dedicate the future of that love to him.

Similarly, if God is the creator of life, and he gives to parents the joy, responsibility and privilege of sharing in that creation, then our first reaction will be to recognize and celebrate the Divine in the life of a baby. Following on from this can come discussions concerning the meaning and place of baptism and membership of the believing community. Unconditional love requires unconditional acceptance of the life-giving energies of God, and of the presence of Christ in the lives of all people. If all life is imbued with the presence of the cosmic Christ, then both baptized members of the Church and those who are unbaptized will bring him into the church with them. The difference between the two will be more to do with where they are on their journey of faith rather than whether they are 'in' or 'out'.

If a priest is to participate in the prayer of the world, then wherever that prayer surfaces in the lives of others, it should be taken seriously and granted its own integrity. The legitimate aspirations of society have always mattered to the Church. They do not become illegitimate because they come from non-ecclesiastical backgrounds and are concerned with the material provisions of life. (We have already noted that it is a false definition to differentiate between the physical and spiritual.) Here the task of the spiritual leader is to make others aware that repentance involves a realization that an over-reliance on the things of this world – used as ends in themselves and for selfish gratification alone – is likely to divert them from true spiritual growth and development.

To be involved in the prayer of the world is to be unashamedly involved in its legitimate aspirations. And what do people pray for? They ask for food, clothing, housing, good education for their children, job security, the ability to keep paying the mortgage and so on. They also pray for peace, safety and help in times of trouble and in particular for themselves and their loved ones when the pain of grief tears their hearts in two. All these are spiritual concerns in which the priest is called to laugh and cry with the world.

All this, and much of what has gone before, may appear to represent an impossible calling for anyone to fulfil. James and John appear undaunted at the time by the answers that Christ gave to their original question on the road to Jerusalem. They remain attentive and completely committed as the road takes them to the foot of the cross. Given their determination, ambition, rugged faith and close friendship, it comes as a surprise that they are both absent when Jesus gave a 'loud cry and breathed his last' (Mark 15.37). At the request of Jesus (John 19.26–27), John was caring for Mary, but the Gospels give no indication as to the whereabouts of James. The women who remained, however (Mark 15.40), no doubt recounted in great detail the final, aweful moments and somewhere in that story may have been the last words that Luke records for us: 'Father, into your hands I commend my spirit' (Luke 23.46, quoting Psalm 31.5). Whether Jesus uttered these words from Psalm 31 in a final lucid moment prior to death as an expression of his faith in God, or whether these have been added later as a testament of faith by the early Christian community, is a matter for honest debate. Nevertheless, the appearance of these words at this point is of great significance. They will no doubt have become a prayer treasured by James and John and were certainly used by the Church from the first century onwards. They remind us first of the need to pray constantly, to remember that the love of God is gentle and always dependable. In addition, they confirm that in all our endeavours 'begun, continued and ended in him', we never walk or work alone. They remind us above all that journey's end is but journey's beginning.

NOTES

1 cf. V. Donovan, *The Church in the Midst of Creation*, SCM Press, London, 1989, p. 119.
2 cf. L. Thunberg, *Man and the Cosmos: The Vision of St Maximus the Confessor*, St Vladimir's Seminary Press, 1985, pp. 131–43.
3 Mark 4.39, cf. Mark 1.25 (φιμοω: lit. to close the mouth with a muzzle).
4 cf. M. Fox, *Original Blessing*, Bear and Co., 1983, pp. 48–9.

REFERENCES

Mother Mary Clare, *Encountering the Depths*, SLG Press, Oxford, 1981, p. 69.

A PRAYER FOR THE START OF THE DAY

Heavenly Father,
Grant me grace to fulfil my calling by following your way
of incarnate love
that I might make you known to those I seek to serve in
your name.
Take me, break me, give me
that I might tell others of the journey
and share with them your food for the way
so that they will come to you
and we will live
for ever.

†

So grant me peace, perseverance, protection from evil and
the enduring love of Christ
for ever.

†

Time for repentance and the patience and comfort of the
Holy Spirit.

†

And may joyful obedience in your service be mine for ever.
Lord, as thou wilt and as thou knowest best.
have mercy*
in Jesus' name.
Amen.

AC

---

* They asked Abba Macarius, 'How should one pray?' The old man replied,
'There is no need to lose oneself in words. It is enough to spread out the hands
and to say, "Lord, as thou wilt and as thou knowest best, have mercy."'
From *Sayings of the Desert Fathers*, Macarius, 19 (PG 65,269), quoted by
Olivier Clément in *The Roots of Christian Mysticism*, New City, 1993, p. 203.

The Society for Promoting Christian Knowledge (SPCK) was founded in 1698. Its mission statement is:

To promote Christian knowledge by

- **Communicating the Christian faith in its rich diversity**

- **Helping people to understand the Christian faith and to develop their personal faith; and**

- **Equipping Christians for mission and ministry**

SPCK Worldwide serves the Church through Christian literature and communication projects in 100 countries, and provides books for those training for ministry in many parts of the developing world. This worldwide service depends upon the generosity of others and all gifts are spent wholly on ministry programmes, without deductions.

SPCK Bookshops support the life of the Christian community by making available a full range of Christian literature and other resources, providing support for those training for ministry, and assisting bookstalls and book agents throughout the UK.

SPCK Publishing produces Christian books and resources, covering a wide range of inspirational, pastoral, practical and academic subjects. Authors are drawn from many different Christian traditions, and publications aim to meet the needs of a wide variety of readers in the UK and throughout the world.

The Society does not necessarily endorse the individual views contained in its publications, but hopes they stimulate readers to think about and further develop their Christian faith.

For information about the Society, visit our website at *www.spck.org.uk*, or write to:
SPCK, Holy Trinity Church, Marylebone Road,
London NW1 4DU, United Kingdom.